ᐃᓄᐃᑦ ᓴᓇᕐᑐᖕᒥᑦ ᓴᓇᔪᓯᖕᒥᓪᓗ
ᐱᑎᒋᐊᖁᓂᖅ 1

INUIT TOOLS AND TECHNIQUES SERIES
VOLUME 1

ᐃᒡᓗᓯᓂᖅ
ᖃᒧᑎᕆᐅᕐᓂᓕ

How To Build an Iglu and a Qamutiik

ᓱᓗᒧᓐ ᐊᐳ
Solomon Awa

ᐊᓐᑐᑦᕈᓴᕝᐳ
Andrew Breithaupt

INHABIT
M E D I A

W0082086

Published by Inhabit Media Inc.
Nunavut Office - P.O. Box 11125, Iqaluit, Nunavut X0A 1HO
Ontario Office - 146A Orchard View Blvd., Toronto, Ontario M4R 1C3
www.inhabitmedia.com

Written by Solomon Awa
Translated by Saa Pitseolak and Louise Flaherty
Edited by Louise Flaherty
Photographs by B&C Alexander/Arcticphoto, Ron Wassink, and Nunavut Tourism
Illustrations by Andrew Breithaupt

We acknowledge the support of the Canada Council for the Arts for our publishing program.

Printed and bound in Canada.

Library and Archives Canada Cataloguing in Publication

Awa, Solomon, 1959-
    Igluvigaliurniq qamusiurnirlu = How to build an iglu & a
qamutiik / Solomon Awa ; [illustrated by] Andrew Breithaupt.

Title in Inuktitut romanized: Igluvigaliurniq qamusiurnirlu.
Parallel English and Inuktitut text.
ISBN 978-1-927095-31-7

    1. Igloos--Design and construction--Juvenile literature.
2. Sleds--Arctic regions--Design and construction--Juvenile
literature. 3. Wilderness survival--Arctic regions--Juvenile
literature. I. Breithaupt, Andrew II. Title. III. Title: How to
build an iglu & a qamutiik.

TH4890.A92 2013   j693'.91   C2013-901180-3

ᕿᑭᖅᑕᓂ ᐃᓄᐃᑦ ᑲᑐᔨᖃᑎᒌᖏᑦ
Qikiqtani Inuit Association

Nunavut

Canada Council   Conseil des Arts
for the Arts   du Canada

Canadä

Canadian   Patrimoine
Heritage   canadien

ᐃᓄᐃᑦ ᓴᓇᕐᑭᑎᖏᑦ ᓴᓇᔾᔪᓯᖏᓪᓗ
ᐱᓕᓇᐊᖑᓂᖅ 1

INUIT TOOLS AND TECHNIQUES SERIES
VOLUME 1

ᐃᒡᓗᓕᓂᖅ ᖃᒪᓯᐅᕐᓂᕐᓗ

How To Build an Iglu and a Qamutiik

ᓵᓗᒫᓂ ᐊᕙ
Solomon Awa

ᐋᓐᑐᕉᕗᕋᐃᑕᑉ
Andrew Breithaupt

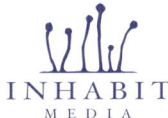

INHABIT MEDIA

ᖃᐅᔨᑎᑦᑎᒋᐊᕈᑎ

ᕿᑭᖅᑕᓂ ᐃᓄᐃᑦ ᑲᑐᔾᔨᖃᑎᒌᒃᑯᑦ ᕿᒥᕐᕈᐊᒐᕋᓛᓕᐅᓚᐅᖅᐳᑦ ᑖᒃᓱᒥᖓ ᖃᐅᔨᒪᔾᔪᑎᒋᔭᐅᖃᑦᑕᕐᓂᐊᕐᒪᑦ ᐃᓄᐃᑦ ᓴᓇᕐᕈᑎᖏᓐᓂᒃ ᓴᓇᔾᔪᓯᖏᓐᓂᑦᓗ ᓴᓇᔭᐅᓚᐅᖅᑐᓂᒃ ᐊᕙᓗᒥᐅᑕᕐᓂᒃ ᑭᖑᓕᕇᓂᒃ ᓄᓇᕗᒻᒥᑦ ᒪᕐᕈᖕᓂᒃ ᐅᖃᐅᓯᓕᖕᓄᑦ ᑲᑐᔾᔨᖃᑎᒌᓄᑦ 2006ᒥ. ᑖᒃᑯᐊ ᓴᓇᔭᐅᓚᐅᕐᒪᑕ ᓴᖅᑮᓇᓱᐊᖅᑐᑎᒃ ᐊᔾᔨᐅᖏᓐᓂᖏᓐᓂᒃ ᓴᓇᑐᓂᖏᓐᓂᑦᓗ ᑲᓇᑕᐅᑉ ᑲᓇᖕᓇᖓᑕ ᐃᓄᖏᑕ – ᑕᒪᒃᑭᑲᓴᒃᑐᑎᒃ ᓴᓇᔭᐅᓚᐅᖅᓯᒪᔪᑦ ᐊᕐᕌᒍᒐᓵᓗᐃᑦ ᐊᓂᒍᖅᑐᑦ ᑭᖑᓂᑦᑎᓐᓂ ᓴᓇᕐᕈᑎᖃᖅᑎᓐᓇᒥᑦ ᑲᑉᐳᔾᔭᖅᑐᓂᒃ, ᐱᓕᕆᕕᒋᔭᕐᓂᖏᑦᑐᒦᑦᑐᑎᒃ ᐊᑐᐃᓐᓇᖃᑦᑎᐊᕋᑎᒡᓗ ᓴᓈᒃᓴᓂᒃ.

ᑖᒃᑯᐊ ᑭᖑᓕᕇᑦ ᑲᔪᓯᔪᓐᓇᕐᓴᓚᐅᖏᑦᑐᑦ ᐃᑲᔪᓚᐅᖏᑉᐸᑦ ᖃᐅᔨᒪᓂᕐᒥᓄᑦ, ᑲᔪᖏᕐᓂᖓᓄᑦᓗ, ᓲᓗᒨᓂ ᐊᕙ. ᖁᔭᓕᔪᒪᒋᕙᕗᑦᑕᐅᖅ ᐃᓐᓇᐃᑦ ᐱᖃᑕᐅᓚᐅᖅᑐᑦ ᖃᐅᔨᒪᓂᕐᒥᑎᒍᑦᓗ ᐃᑲᔪᑦᑕᐅᑎᒋᔪᓐᓇᓚᐅᖅᑐᑦ ᑖᒃᓱᒥᖓ ᐱᓕᕆᐊᖃᖅᑎᑦᓗᑕ. ᑎᑎᖅᑐᒐᖅᑎ ᐋᓐᑐᕉ ᕗᓴᐃᑕᑉ ᐱᓕᕆᑦᑎᐊᖅᑐᐊᓘᓚᐅᖅᑐᖅ ᑎᑎᖅᑐᒐᖅᑕᖏᑎᒍᑦ ᑕᑯᓐᓇᕐᓗᒍᓗ ᐃᓕᓐᓂᐊᕈᑎᑦᑎᐊᕙᐅᓕᖅᑎᑦᑐᓂᐅᒃ.

ᑐᑭᓯᑎᑦᓯᔾᔪᑦ

ᒥᑦᓯᒪᑕᓕᒻᒥ ᐱᕈᖅᓴᑦᓗᖓ ᐃᒡᓗᕕᒐᓕᐅᖃᑦᑕᓯᓚᐅᖅᓯᒪᔪᖓ ᖃᒧᑎᓂᑦᓗ ᒥᑭᔫᑦᓯᖓ,ᐊᑖᑕᒐᓗ ᐅᕙᒍᒃ. ᐊᑖᑕᒪ ᐃᓕᓐᓂᐊᖅᑎᒍᒪᓚᐅᖅᓯᒪᒻᒫᖓ ᐃᓄᐃᑦ ᐃᓕᖅᑯᓯᖏᓐᓂᒃ, ᐃᓕᓐᓂᐊᕆᐊᕐᑯᙱᖕᒫᖅᓯᖓ ᐃᓕᓐᓂᐊᕐᕕᒻᒧᑦ. ᑕᐃᒪᙵᓂᒃ ᐃᓕᕝᕕᒋᓯᓚᐅᖅᑕᕋ ᐊᒥᓱᓂᒃ ᐃᓄᐃᑦ ᓴᓇᕐᕈᑎᖏᓐᓂᒃ ᐱᔾᔪᓯᖏᓐᓂᑦᓗ- ᓴᓇᙳᐊᕐᓂᒃᑯᑦ ᓴᓇᓂᒃᑯᑦᓗ. ᐊᓈᓇᒪ ᐃᓕᓐᓂᐊᖅᑎᓚᐅᖅᓯᒪᒻᒥᔮᖓ ᖃᓄᑐᐃᓐᓇᑦᓯᐊᖅ, ᐊᑦᓛᑦ ᒥᖅᓱᕐᓂᕐᒥᒃ. ᐊᖏᕐᕋᕗᑦ ᐃᓕᓐᓂᐊᕕᒋᓚᐅᖅᑕᕋ. ᐃᒡᓗᓕᒋᐅᖅᓴᕈᓐᓇᖅᑐᑎᑦ ᐅᑦᓗᓂᒃ ᐊᒥᓲᙱᑦᑐᓂᒃ, ᑭᓯᐊᓂ ᓴᓇᑦᓯᐊᖅᓯᑕᐅᓂᐊᕐᓗᓂ ᐱᓴᕆᐅᖅᓴᕆᐊᓕᒃ ᐊᒥᓱᐊᖅᑎᐊᓗᒃ. ᐱᓗᐊᖅᑐᒥ ᐊᐳᑦ ᓴᓇᒐᓱᐊᕐᓗᒍ. ᐊᐳᑎᐅᑉ ᖃᓄᐃᑦᑑᓂᖏᑦ ᐊᔾᔨᒌᒍᓐᓇᖏᑦᑐᑦ ᓇᒥᓕᒫᖅ; ᓰᕐᓗ...ᐊᓄᕆᐅᑉ ᓇᑭᙶᕐᓂᖓ ᓴᓇᑦᓚᕆᒻᒪᑦ ᐊᐳᑎᐅᑉ ᖃᓄᐃᓐᓂᖓᓂᒃ. ᓇᒥ ᐃᒡᓗᓕᓂᐊᕐᒪᖔᖅᐱᑦ ᖃᐅᔨᒪᑦᓯᐊᕆᐊᖃᕐᒥᔪᑎᑦ- ᓂᕕᖓᔪᖃᙱᒃᑲᓗᐊᕐᒪᖔᑦ ᖃᐅᔨᓴᕆᐊᖃᖅᑐᑎᑦ, ᐊᐳᒻᒥᒃ, ᓯᑑᕋᕐᕕᐅᑦᑕᕈᐊᕋᕕᑦ. ᖃᐅᔨᒪᓃᑦ ᓇᒦᒻᒪᖔᖅᐱᑦ ᑖᓐᓇ ᐱᒻᒪᕆᐅᒻᒪᑦ. ᐅᑦᓗᒥᐅᓕᖅᑐᖅ ᐃᒡᓗᕕᒐᐃᑦ ᓴᓇᔭᐅᖃᑦᑕᓕᖅᑐᑦ ᖁᕕᐊᓱᒍᑕᐅᑦᓱᑎᒃ ᓵᓚᖃᕈᑕᐅᒐᓱᐊᖅᓱᑎᑦᓗ, ᓱᓕ ᐃᓛᓐᓂᒃᑯᑦ ᓴᓇᔭᐅᓲᑦ ᐊᑑᑎᑦᓚᕆᖏᓐᓄᑦ ᐊᓐᓇᐅᒪᔭᕆᐊᖃᕐᓂᕐᒧᑦ. ᐊᓐᓇᓐᓂᐊᕈᓂ ᓇᒥᑐᐃᓐᓇᖅ ᐃᓄᒃ ᖃᐅᔨᒪᑦᓯᐊᕆᐊᖃᖅᑯᖅ ᓇᒥ ᐆᒪᔪᖅᓯᐅᕐᓂᐊᕐᒪᖔᕐᒥ, ᓇᒧᙵᕆᐊᖃᕐᒪᖔᕐᒥ ᖃᒧᑕᐅᔭᐃᑦᑕᒍᓂ, ᐅᖅᓱᐃᕈᔾᔭᒍᓂ, ᐊᓯᐊᒍᑦᓘᓐᓃᑦ.

ᖃᒧᑏᑦ ᐊᔾᔨᒌᖑᙱᒻᒥᔪᑦ ᓄᓇᓕᓐᓂ. ᓲᕐᓗ ᐃᖃᓗᓐᓂ, ᒪᓃᑦᑐᐹᓗᒃ. ᐊᕐᕕᐊᑦ ᒪᓂᕐᑦᑎᑦᑐᒍ. ᑕᒪᓐᓇ ᐱᑦᑐᒍ ᐊᔾᔨᒌᖑᙱᓚᑦ ᓴᓇᔭᐅᓂᖏᑦ ᑕᐅᑦᑐᖏᑦᑐ. ᑐᓄᓂᕈᓯᕐᒥ/ᐃᒃᐱᐊᕐᔪᒃ, ᓴᓂᕐᔭᒻᒥ, ᒥᑦᔨᒪᑕᓕᒻᒥ, ᑲᖏᖅᓲᓚᐱᒻᒥᓗᖃᐃ ᖃᒧᑏᑦ ᐊᖏᓂᖅᓴᐃᑦ. ᑕᐃᒪᐃᑦᑐᑦ ᓯᑯᒃᑰᕐᓂᖅᓴᐅᖃᑦᑕᕐᖓᑕ. ᐃᖃᓗᓐᓂ ᖃᒧᑏᑦ ᒪᓃᑦᑐᒃᑰᕈᑕᐅᓂᖅᓴᐃᑦ ᓄᓇᒃᑯᑦ, ᓴᖑᖓᓂᖅᑲᖅᓯᑎᒃ ᐊᒻᒧᐊᖓᓂᖅᑲᖅᓯᑎᑦᑐ. ᐊᒥᓐᓂᖅᓴᐅᕆᐊᖅᑲᖅᓯᑎᒃ, ᓂᕈᑭᓐᓂᖅᓴᐅᓗᑎᒃ ᐊᒻᒪᓗ ᓇᐃᓐᓂᖅᓴᐅᒻᒥᓗᑎᒃ. ᓯᓚᐅᑉ ᓇᑦᓕᐅᓐᓂᖏᑦ ᐊᑦᓛᑦ ᒪᓕᒃᑕᐅᓲᑦ ᖃᒧᓯᐅᖅᑐᓄᑦ; ᐅᑭᐅᖅᓯᐅᑏᒃ ᐊᔾᔨᒋᔾᔫᙱᑕᖏᒃ ᐅᐱᕐᖔᖅᓯᐅᑎᐅᑉ. ᓴᓇᓂᐊᕈᕕᑦ ᖃᒧᑏᓐᓂᒃ ᐱᐅᓂᖅᓴᖅ ᐃᓄᓐᓄᑦ ᐅᖃᓕᒪᒍᕕᑦ ᓄᓇᓕᒻᒥ, ᐊᒻᒪᓗ ᓄᓇᖓ ᖃᓄᐃᑦᑕᕐᒪᖔᑦ ᐃᑉᐱᒋᒐᓱᐊᕐᓗᒍ. ᑐᑭᓯᓂᐊᕐᕕᑦ ᖃᓄᕐᓕ ᐊᖑᓇᓱᖃᑦᑕᕐᒪᖔᑕ.

ᐃᓄᐃᑦ ᐃᓚᖏᑦ ᖃᒧᓯᐅᕐᓂᐊᕋᒥᒃ ᓂᕈᐊᓲᖑᒻᒥᔪᑦ ᖃᒧᑎᒃᓴᕐᓂᒃ ᕿᔪᓐᓂᒃ- ᑕᒪᓐᓇ ᑐᕌᖓᒻᒥᔪᖅ ᓄᓇᓕᓐᓄᑦ. ᐃᓚᖏᑦ ᕿᔪᑐᐃᓐᓇᕐᓂᒃ ᐱᐅᒃᓴᖅᑐᑦ, ᐊᒥᓲᑦᓗᑕᓂ ᐱᐅᒃᓴᕐᓂᖅᓴᐅᔪᒍᑦ ᓯᑎᓂᖅᓴᒥᒃ ᕿᔪᒻᒥᒃ. ᓯᑎᔪᑦ ᓴᙱᓂᖅᓴᐅᒻᒪᑕ ᐱᐅᑦᓗᓂᓗ ᕿᑐᓐᓂᖅᓴᐅᒻᒪᑦ. ᐊᑲᐅᓂᖅᓴᐅᓚᕿᕗᖅ ᐊᖑᓇᓱᑦᓗᓂ. ᖃᒧᑎᐅᑉ ᓴᓇᒪᓂᖓ ᓴᓇᔭᐅᔫᖅ ᓇᒦᓐᓃᑦ ᒪᓕᑦᓯᒍ. ᓈᒻᒪᑦᓯᐊᓇᐊᖃᖅᑲᑦ ᐃᖏᕐᕋᑦᓯᐊᕐᓂᖓ ᐅᕿᓐᓂᖓᓗ, ᐊᑑᑎᒋᒻᒪᒋᒃ. ᐅᓇ ᐃᓱᒪᒋᓯᐅᒃ, ᓇᒻᒪᒍᓐᓇᕐᕕᑦ ᐆᖅᑲᑦᓯᐊᖅᓯᒪᔪᒥᒃ ᐅᖁᒪᐃᑦᑐᒥᒃ, ᐱᓱᑦᓗᑎᒃ ᐅᖓᓯᒃᑐᒧᑦ ᐃᓱᒪᒋᙱᑦᓯᐊᕐᓗᒍ ᐅᖁᒪᐃᒋᐊᖓ. ᑕᐃᒫᑦᓗᐊᖅ ᐅᖁᒪᐃᓐᓂᓕᒻᒥᒃ ᐆᖅᑲᑦᓯᐊᖅᓯᒪᙱᑦᑐᒥᒃ ᓇᒻᒪᒍᑦ, ᐃᑉᐱᒋᓚᖓᔭᐃᑦ ᐅᖁᒪᐃᓐᓂᖓ ᐱᓱᒋᐊᓯᑐᐊᕈᕕᑦ.

ᐅᓇ ᐅᖃᓕᒫᒐᖅ ᐃᑲᔫᑎᒃᓴᖅ ᖃᓄᖅ ᓴᓇᒋᐊᖃᕐᒪᖔᖅᐱᑦ ᑖᒃᑯᓃᖓ ᒪᖀᓐᓂᒃ, ᐱᑦᓚᓈᓐᓂᒃ ᐃᓄᐃᑦ ᐃᓕᖅᑯᓯᑐᖃᖏᓐᓄᑦ. ᐃᒡᓗᕕᒐᓕᒍᓐᓇᖅᑐᖓ ᖃᒧᓯᐅᕐᓗᖓᓗ ᐊᑖᑕᒪ ᐃᓕᓐᓂᐊᖅᑎᓚᐅᖅᓯᒪᒻᒫᖓ. ᖃᐅᔨᒪᓂᖃᓗ ᐊᓯᓐᓄᑦ ᐊᐃᑦᓲᑎᒋᒋᐊᖃᕐᒥᔭᕐ, ᐱᐅᓯᓇᒐᑦᑎᒍ. ᑕᒪᒃᑯᐊ ᐳᐃᒍᖅᑕᐅᖁᙱᑕᒃᑲ. ᐃᓕᓐᓂᐊᑎᑦᓯᔾᔪᑎᒌᓐᓇᕈᑦᑎᒍ, ᐊᑯᓂᐅᓂᖅᓴᖅ ᐸᐸᑕᐅᓂᐊᖅᑐᑦ ᐃᓄᓐᓄᑦ-ᐃᓕᓐᓂᐊᑎᑦᓯᔾᔪᑎᒋᖃᑦᑕᖏᒃᑯᑦᑎᒍ, ᐊᓯᐅᓂᐊᖅᑐᑦ.

- ᓲᓗᒨᓂ ᐊᕚ

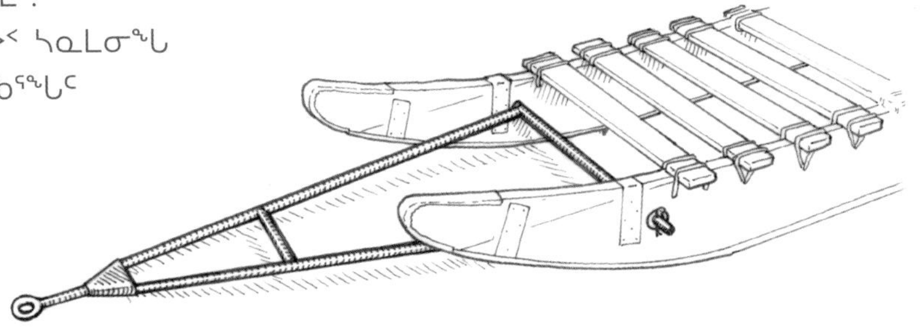

PREFACE

The Qikiqtani Inuit Association developed this booklet as a portable reference guide to complement the original Inuit Tools and Techniques Poster Series developed by the Nunavut Bilingual Education Society in 2006. This series was designed to capture the uniqueness and ingenuity displayed in items invented by eastern Canadian Inuit—most of which were developed years ago in harsh conditions with limited materials.

This series would not have been possible without the knowledge, motivation, and skills of Solomon Awa. We would also like to thank the elders who participated and readily contributed their vast knowledge to this project. Illustrator Andrew Breithaupt did an amazing job with the artwork and made this series a dynamic visual learning tool.

Tony Romito

INTRODUCTION

Growing up in Pond Inlet, I started to build iglus and qamutiiks with my father at a young age. My father wanted to teach me traditional knowledge, instead of putting me into a modern school system, so I apprenticed him in learning many traditional tools and techniques, from carving to building. My mother taught me many skills as well, including sewing. Home was my school.

You can learn to build an iglu in a few days, but to become really skilled, it will take a lot of practice, especially when it comes to working with snow. Snow conditions vary from location to location; for example, wind direction has a strong impact on the quality of the snow. Choosing a site on which to build the iglu is very important, too—you have to make sure there is no overhang, no snow above, and no risk of an avalanche. Generally, being aware of the geography of the area you're in is crucial. While iglus today are often built for fun and contests, they are sometimes still built for their traditional purpose of survival, and in order to survive in an area one must know where to hunt, where to go if your snowmobile breaks down or runs out of gas, and so on.

Qamutiiks are very different in different communities. For instance, Iqaluit is very rough, while Arviat is flat. This has a big impact on the design and style of the qamutiiks in each area. In Arctic Bay, Hall Beach, Iglulik, Pond Inlet, and perhaps Clyde River, the qamutiiks are larger, because they're mostly travelling across ice. In Iqaluit, qamutiiks mostly have to travel across rough land with inclines and declines, so they have to be much thinner, narrower, and shorter. There are also different kinds of qamutiiks based on season; winter qamutiiks will vary from spring qamutiiks. It is critical when thinking about building a qamutiik to first look around and talk to the people in the community to see how they deal with their hunting.

Some people have preferences when it comes to wood for their qamutiik—this also depends on the community. Some people prefer plain spruce wood, while most of us prefer hardwood. It is more flexible and stronger, and as a result is better for hunting. The shape of the qamutiik depends on where you are. The shape has to be perfect in order for the qamutiik to be smooth or light, which is the goal. Take this example. You can carry a well-fitting backpack with fifty pounds in it, and walk a long distance without thinking you are carrying fifty pounds. But if you have the same amount of weight in an ill-fitting backpack, you will be aware of the weight from your first step.

This book is a guide to building these two items, both being vital elements of traditional Inuit lifestyles. I know how to make iglus and qamutiiks because my father passed the knowledge along to me, and it is important for me to continue to pass the knowledge along. I don't want these things to be forgotten. If we keep teaching them, they will last longer—if we stop teaching them, they will fade away.

Solomon Awa

ᐃᒡᓗ IGLU

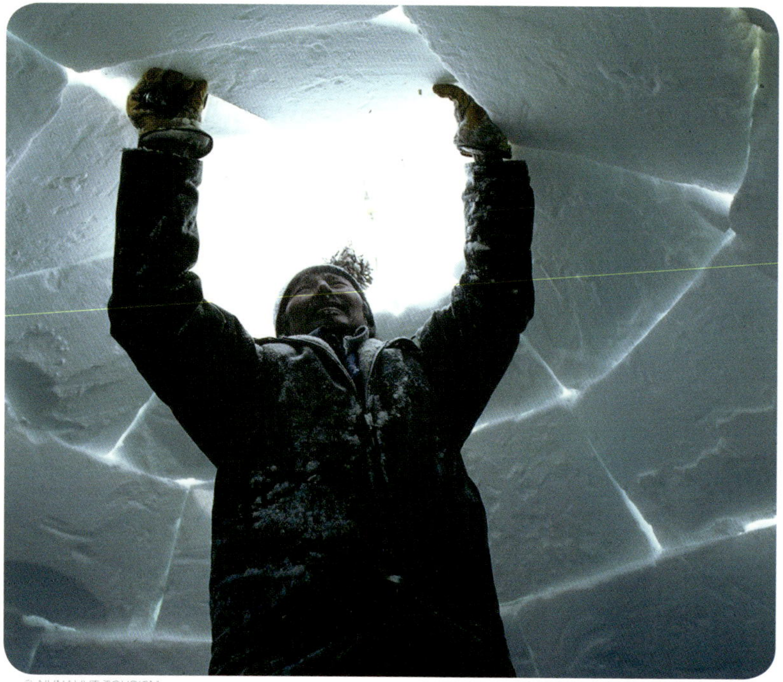

© NUNAVUT TOURISM

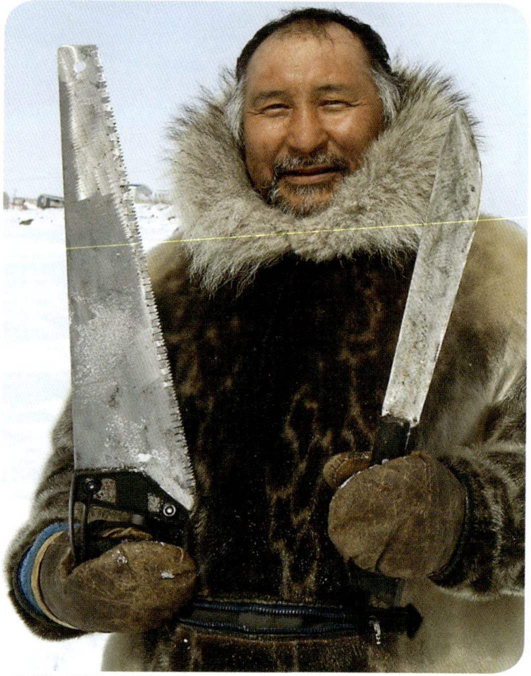

© RON WASSINK

ᐅᖃᖅᑕᐅᔭᖐᓐᒪᑦ ᐃᒡᓗ ᐅᕝᕙᓘᓐᓃᑦ ᐃᒡᓗ ᑐᑭᓯᔭᐅᔪᓐᓇᖅᑦᑕᖅᑐᖅ ᖃᓪᓗᓈᓄᑦ, ᑲᓇᑕᐅᑉ ᖁᑦᑎᖕᓂᐊᓃᑦᑐᓄᑦ ᐃᓄᖕᓄᑦ ᐊᑐᖅᑕᐅᔪᑐᖅᑲᖅ ᐅᖅᑯᐃᔾᔪᑕᐅᕙᒃᓗᓂ. ᐊᐅᓪᓛᖅᑐᓄᓪᓘᓐᓃᑦ ᐊᖑᓇᓱᒋᐊᖅᑐᓄᓪᓘᓐᓃᑦ ᐅᓐᓄᐊᖕᒋᓐᓈᖅᓂᐊᖐᓐᒪᑕᓗ ᐊᑐᖅᑕᐅᓲᖑᔪᑦ. ᒥᑭᓈᖅᑕᐅᒐᔪᒃᑐᑦ ᑭᓯᐊᓂᓚᑦᑕᐅᖅ ᐊᖏᔪᐊᓘᑎᑕᐅᔪᓐᓇᖅᒥᔪᑦ (ᖃᒡᒋᕕᓕᐊᖑᓗᑎᒃ) ᐊᔾᔨᐅᖏᑦᑐᓕᓂᐊᖐᓐᒪᒥᒃ.

The iglu, or "igloo," as it is commonly known in the South, is a traditional winter shelter built by the Inuit of Canada's North. These shelters are generally temporary and are used for overnight hunting and travelling expeditions. Most iglus are small but could be made very large (a qaggivik) for special events or gatherings.

ᖃᐅᔨᒪᔭᐅᓂᖓ

ᐱᔪᓐᓇᑦᑎᐊᖅᑐᑦ ᐃᒡᓗᓕᐅᓲᖑᔪᑦ ᐊᑦᑕᕐᓇᖏᑦᑐᒥᒃ ᐅᖅᑰᑦᑎᐊᖅᑐᒥᒡᓗ ᓂᒡᓚᓱᒃᑐᒥᐅᑕᐅᔪᓄᑦ. ᓴᓇᑦᑎᐊᖅᓯᒪᔭᕌᖓᒥᒃ ᐅᖅᑰᑦᑎᐊᕈᓐᓇᖃᑦᑕᖅᑐᑦ ᓂᒡᓚᓱᒃᑐᒻᒪᕆᐅᒐᓗᐊᖅᑎᓪᓗᒍ.

ᐊᐳᑎᑐᐃᓐᓇᕐᒥᑦ ᐊᐅᕕᒃᓴᓕᐅᖅᑐᖅᑲᕈᓐᓇᖏᑦᑐᖅ. ᐊᐳᑦ ᑎᓵᖓᑦᑎᐊᕆᐊᖃᕐᒪᑦ, ᐊᔾᔨᒌᑦᑎᐊᕐᓗᓂᓗ ᑎᓯᓗᐊᖏᑦᑐᓂᓗ. ᐊᐳᑦ ᑎᓯᓗᐊᕌᖓᑦ ᐅᑦᓯᓗᐊᕋᔭᕐᒪᑦ ᓂᒡᓚᓱᖕᓂᖅᓴᐅᔭᒃᓗᓂ ᐳᔫᖅᓴᕋᐃᓐᓂᖅᓴᐅᑦᑐᓂᓗ. ᐊᖅᑭᓗᐊᕌᖓᑦᓗ ᐋᖅᑭᑦᑎᐊᕈᓐᓇᕋᓂ ᒪᓐᖑᓯᒐᔪᖕᓂᖅᓴᐅᑦᑐᓂ ᑯᑐᒎᓂᖅᓴᐅᑦᑐᓂᓗ. ᐳᑲᔮᖓᔪᖅ ᐊᐳᑎᓕᖅᑭᒃᑖᖑᖏᑦᑐᓂ (ᐊᓄᕆᒥᑦ ᑕᒫᓐᖓᑦᓴᐃᓐᓇᖅ ᐊᐱᓂᑯ) ᐱᖑᐊᕐᔫᑉ ᓵᑦᑎᐊᖓᓂ ᐱᐅᓂᖅᐹᖑᒐᔪᒃᑐᖅ.

ᖃᐅᔨᒪᔭᕆᐊᖃᓪᓚᕆᒃᑐᖅ ᑲᖏᖃᕆᐊᖃᑦᑐᖅ (ᕿᖓᖃᕆᐊᖃᑦᑐᖅ) ᖁᓪᓕᖃᕐᓂᐊᕈᕕᑦ ᐅᖅᑰᓴᐅᑎᖃᕐᓂᐊᕈᓐᓃᑦ. ᐊᑦᑎᒃᑐᒃᑯᑦ ᐊᖕᒪᓂᖄᕐᔪᒥᐊᖃᖅᑐᖅ ᑲᖏᖃᕐᓗᓂᓗ (ᕿᖓᖃᕐᓗᓂᓗ) ᖁᓚᑦᓗᐊᖓᒎᖏᑦᑐᖅ. ᐅᖅᑰᓯᑎᓗᐊᕆᐊᖃᕐᓂᓗ ᐊᐅᔭᒻᒪᑦ ᐆᓇᔪᒃᑎᑐᐃᓐᓇᕐᓗᒍ ᓈᒻᒪᒃᑐᖅ.

BACKGROUND

It takes a skilled person to make a proper iglu, one that will provide adequate warmth and safety in the Arctic climate. When constructed properly, an iglu can be extremely comfortable, even in the harshest wind and cold.

Snow blocks cannot be cut from just any snowdrift. The snow must be firm, consistent, and not too compacted. If the snow is too hard, there will not be enough air pockets within it, causing the iglu to be colder and more humid. If the snow is too soft, it will not set properly and will tend to slump, bend, and leak very easily. Crystallized snow that has been deposited all at the same time (drifting from a single wind period) on the lee side of a hill is generally the best for making blocks.

It is extremely important to have adequate air flow in an iglu, especially if you are burning a qulliq (a traditional oil lamp) or a modern stove or heater. Make sure that there is a little air entering at the base of the igloo and a vent near the top. It is also important not to overheat your iglu, causing it to melt—the ideal temperature in an iglu is about 1°C.

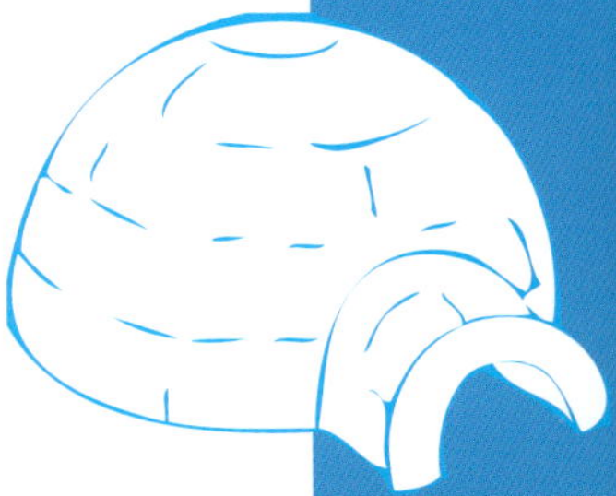

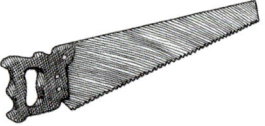

ᐊᐅᐱᖅᓴᕐᓂᖅ
(ᓄᓇᒥ ᐊᐳᑎᑎᐊᓛᖑᓂᕐᒥ)

CUTTING BLOCKS
(ON LAND IN HARD, DEEP DRIFTS)

1

ᐅᑎᖅᑕᖅᐅᖅᖅᑎᑲᐃᐊ ᐊᖅᓗᒍ ᐱᓪᔪᐠᐃᑕ ᐊᐅᐁᑦ ᐱᑎᑲᔪᐊᖅᓰᖅᐃᓯᒍ

Pass your saw through the cut lines several times to make it easier to remove the blocks.

2

ᐊᐅᐁᐊᑦ ᐃᓄᒪᐊᒍᐊᓂᑦ ᐱᖅᐅᕐᓂᐠ ᐃᕐᐊᓂᖅᑲᐊᓂᖅᑐᖅ ᐅᐃᓄᐊᖔᓂᐁᖅᓂᐊᕐᐊᑕ ᐃᕐᐊᓂᖅᓵᐅᖅᐠᖂᓂᐊᒍᐊᖅᑐᖅ ᐊᑯᓂᐅᓂᐊᕐᐊᑕ

Blocks should be three inches thick for a temporary shelter and four or five inches thick for a more permanent shelter.

3

ᓴᓂᕋᖕᑎᑦ ᐊᕿᑎᓚᐅᕐᔪᖕᐠ, ᐊᑕᔪᑦ ᑭᓪᓗᖅᒥᓗᒍ ᐱᒪᐊᖅᓂᐊᕐᐊᒪᑦ

After cutting the sides of the blocks, cut along the bottom.

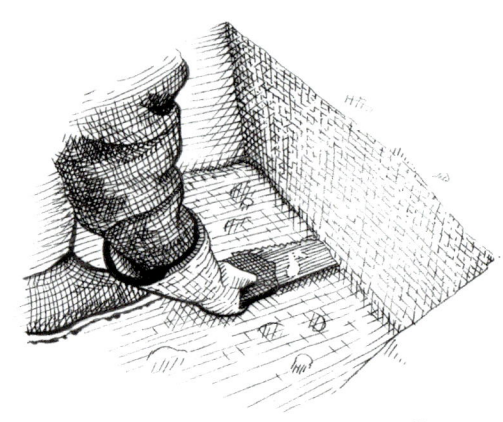

4 ᑭᓪᓘᑏᑦ ᐃᓕᓗᒍ
ᐊᑯᓐᓂᖓᓄᑦ ᐊᐅᕚᑦ
ᓄᓯᒃᔩᒥᓗᒍ ᑐᖏᒧᑦ. ᐸᑎᒃᓗᒍ
ᐊᒃᑲᖕᓄᑦ ᐲᕈᓐᓇᖅᓯᑲᔭᖅᑐᖅ
ᐱᑦᑎᐊᓕᒋᐊᕐᓗᒍ

Slide your saw down the cut line and tilt the block towards you. Grab it with both hands and gently remove it.

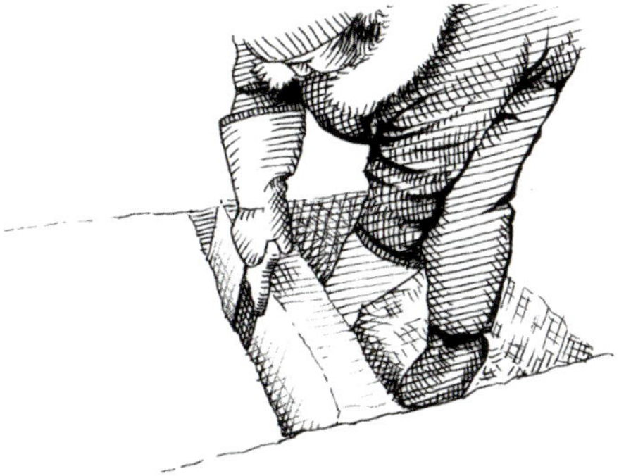

ᓯᑯᒥ ᓘᓐᓃᑦ ᐊᐳᑎᑭᑦᑐᒥᓪᓘᓐᓃᑦ
(ON SEA ICE IN HARD, SHALLOW DRIFTS)

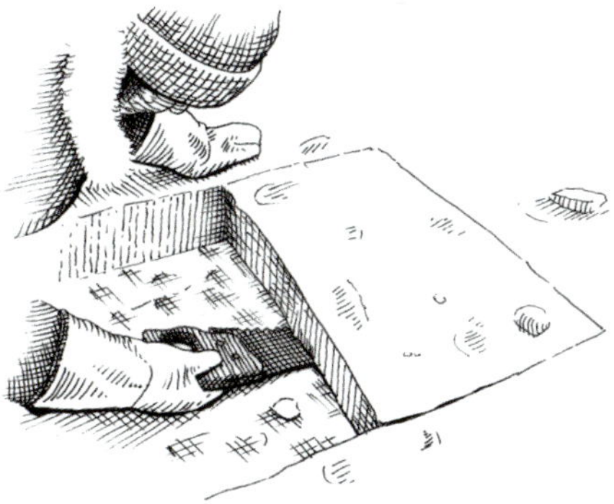

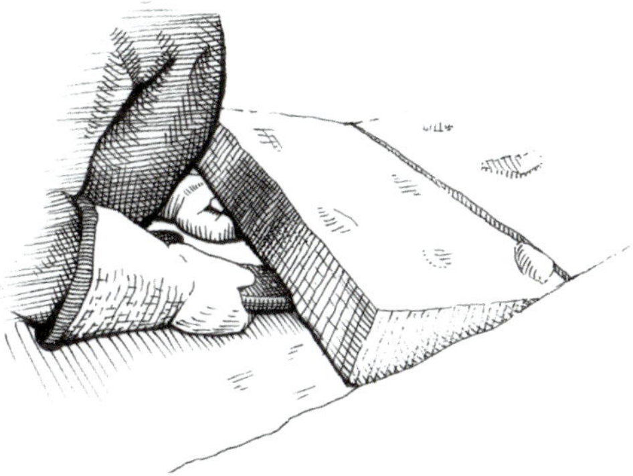

ᐊᐳᑎᑭᓐᓂᕐᒥ ᓯᑯᒥ ᓘᓐᓃᑦ
ᐊᐅᕙᓕᐊᓇᔭᑎᑦ
ᒪᒃᐸᑑᖑᔪᓐᓇᖅᑐᑦ

To build an iglu on the sea ice or in shallow snow, cut your blocks horizontally.

ᐅᔾᔨᕆᓇᑦᑎᐊᕆᐊᖃᖅᑐᖅ
ᖁᐱᓂᖓ
ᐊᔾᔩᒃᑎᒋᐊᕈᓐᓇᖁᓪᓗᒍ

More care must be taken to cut along the bottom of the block to ensure a consistent thickness.

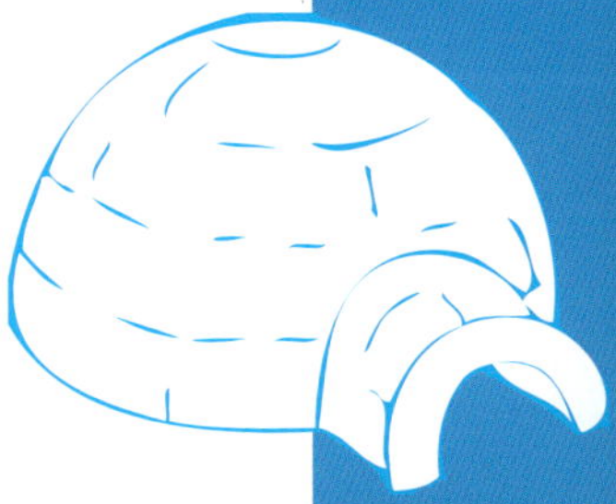

ᑐᵃᖕᓕᐊᒃᓴᖕᓇ
FOUNDATION PREP

ᓴᐱᖕᓄᑦ (ᐸᓇᐅᒡᑦ), ᐃᑭᐊᖅᑎᕐᓗᒍ ᒪᓂᖅᓴᒃ,
ᖃᓴᖕᓂᕐᖅᑎᕐᓗᒍ ᖁᖕᓇ ᑕᒪᕐᓇ ᐊᐅᐱᖅᐱᒃ
ᑐᵃᖕᓕᐊᕆᓂᕐᐊᖅᑕᕐᓇ

With your snow knife, using a horizontal chopping stroke, loosen the top inch of snow where your first row of blocks will rest.

ᐊᕕᓗᐊ
FIRST ROW

ᐊᐅᐱᖅ ᓯᕐᑕᑕᖅᐸᖅ ᐃᓚᓂᖕᒋᕐᓗᒍ ᒪᓂᖅᑳᑦ
ᖁᒃᓗᓇᖕᑲᐹᑕᖅᑎᕐᓗᒍ

Taper the first row of blocks gently from the surface of the snow to create the spiral shape of the iglu.

ᐊᐅᐱᒃᓴᓂᖅ ᐃᓄᖢᖂᖢᓂᖕᑦ
INTERIOR BLOCKS

ᐊᐅᐱᒃᓴᖕᖢᑎᖃᖅᑲᐅᔭᓯᓂᖕᑦ
ᑲᕝᔭᑐᐊᖁᐊᖕᖢᒍ ᐃᓄᐊᓂᖕᑦ
ᐊᕿᐅᖕᔭᑎᓴᔪᖅᐱᖕᓂ ᐃᑦᖢᔪᐱᓯᖢᑦ

Continue cutting blocks from
the inside of the iglu to build the
walls.

ᐊᖅᖅᑲᑎᐊᓄᐊᖅᑲᖕᓂᖕᒪ ᖃᖕᑦᑌᐅᑎᓂᐊᖅᑲᑐᖢᑦ
SURFACE PREP

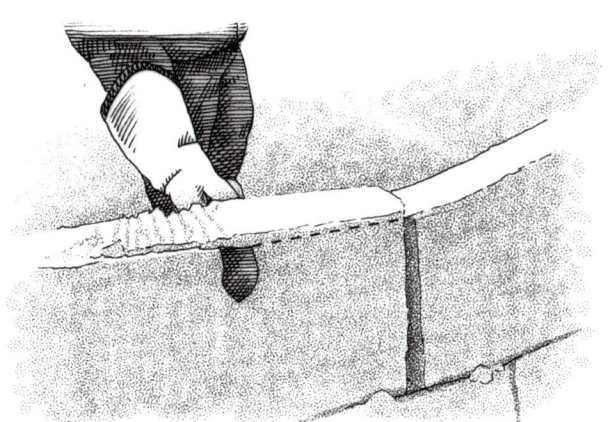

ᒪᓂᖅᑲᖕᔮᒻᖢᒍ ᖃᖕᒪ ᖃᖕᑦᑌᑎᖅᑲᐊᔾᖁᖁᐊᖕᕿᑐᖢᒍ

Smooth off the top edges of the blocks in
preparation for the next layer.

ᐃᒡᓗ IGLU

ᐊᐅᕖᑦ ᐃᓕᐅᖅᑲᕐᓂᖏᑦ
SETTING BLOCKS

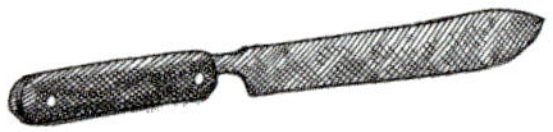

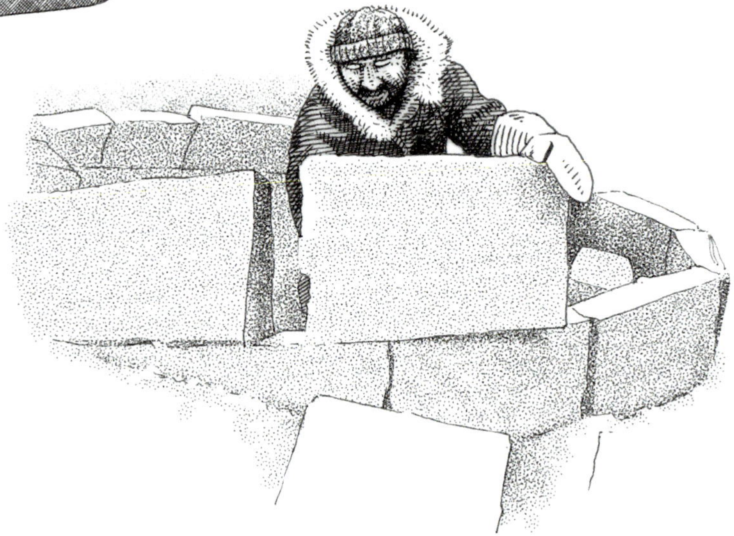

ᐃᓂᖅᑎᑦᑎᓂᖅ ᐊᐅᕕᕐᓂᒃ
ᐅᔾᔨᕆᑦᑎᐊᕆᐊᖅᑲᒪᕆᒃᑐᖅ ᐃᒡᓗᓕᐅᕐᓗᓂ.
ᓇᓗᓇᐃᖅᓯᒪᔪᑦ ᐊᑖᓂ ᐱᔭᕆᐊᖅᑲᕐᓂᖏᑦ

Setting the blocks is the most important part of building the iglu. Follow the steps below to properly set your blocks.

1 ᐊᐅᕕᖅ ᐃᓕᓗᒍ ᓯᒍᑦᑕᐅᖅᑲᐅᔪᒧᑦ ᐊᐳᖅᑎᓪᓗᒍ

Place the new block on the wall and slide it up to the last block you set.

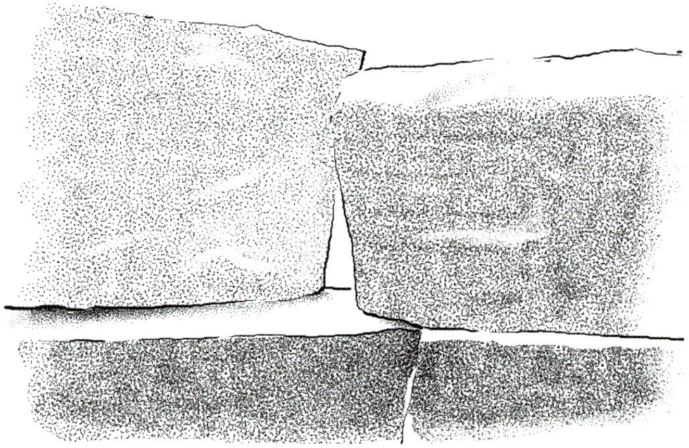

2 ᐃᓚᖑᖕᓯᕐᓗᒍ ᐊᒃᑐᐊᓗᐊᕐᓂᖕᓗᒋᑦ
ᑲᑎᑦᑎᐊᕈᒪᓇᕐᑯᑐᒍ ᐃᒪᖖᓄᑦ

Cut the connecting edge of the new
block to fit the contour of the last
block.

3 ᐃᓚᖑᖕᓯᖅᐸᑦᑕᕐᐊᒍ
ᐅᒻᒪᒃᔭᕋᔭᐊᕐᓂᖕᓯᓂ
ᐊᖅᑲᑎᑦᑎᐊᕈᒪᓇᕐᑯᑐᒍ

Continue to slice your knife
down the connecting edge,
while pushing the new block
into the last one.

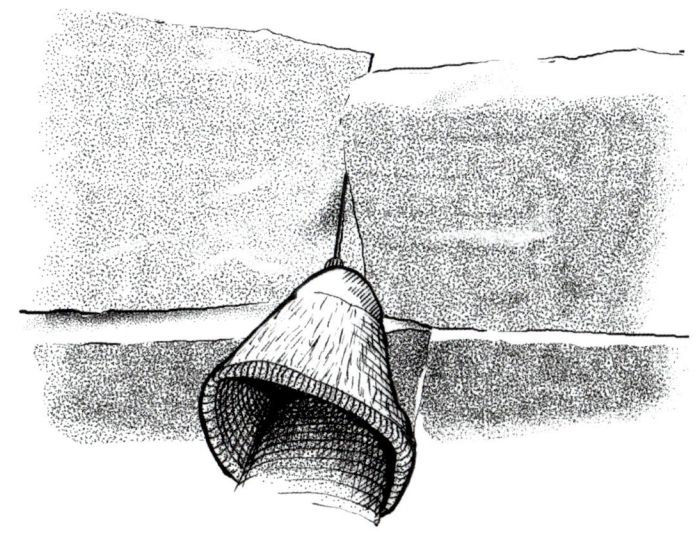

4 ᓴᕕᖕᒧᑦ (ᐸᓇᒧᑦ) ᐊᑖ ᒪᓂᖅᑲᒃᓴᕐᓗᒍ
ᐃᓕᕐᑎᐊᖅᓯᒪᔪᓐᓇᕐᑯᓪᓗᒍ

Use your knife to slice along the bottom of the new block to create a solid joint.

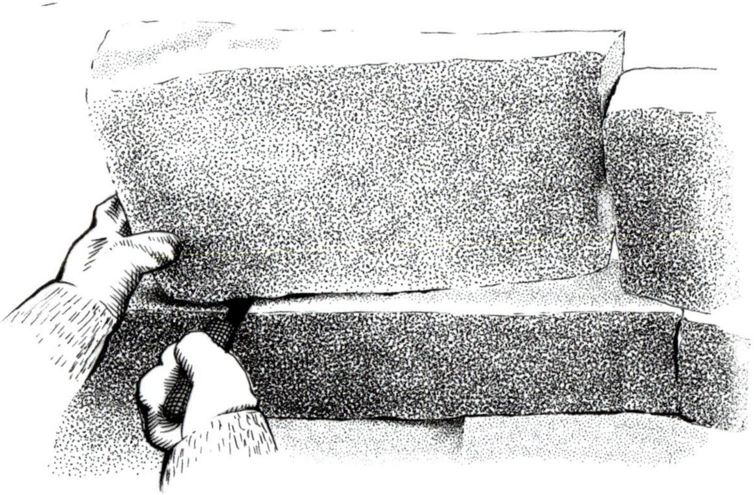

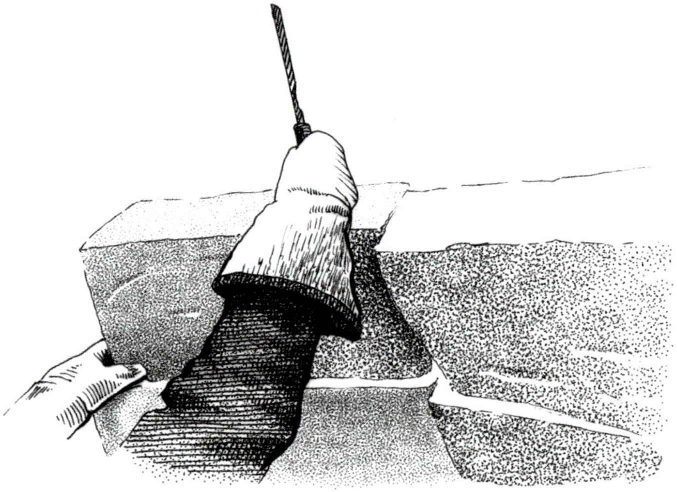

5 ᐊᐅᕕᖅᐱᑦ ᑕᓕᖅᐱᖕᒑᖕᒐᒍᑦ ᐊᒃᒐᖕᖑᑦ ᑲᓯᒃᓗᒍ
ᐊᑦᑕᑕᕈᓐᓇᕐᑯᓪᓗᒍ

Firmly tap down the right side of the block with your hand to position it tightly in the wall.

ᐅᑯᐊᓕᑎᐅᖅᓂᖅ
CUTTING DOOR

ᐅᑯᐊᓕᑎᐅᑉᓄᖅᑐᖅ
ᐱᐊᓂᓕᒪᓂᖅᑲᒃᑐᐊᖅᑎᒡᓗ
ᐃᓯᐅᖅᑲᐃᕋᑎᐊᖅᓂᐊᕐᒋᐊᑦ ᐊᑐᐃᓂᖅ
ᐱᐊᓂᒍᒪᕋᑦᑎᒡᓗ ᐃᑉᑐᑕᐊᓂᔭᐃᑦ

Once three quarters of the iglu is complete, cut the doorway. You may need to bring blocks in through the door to complete the iglu.

ᐊᑐᐃᖅ ᑭᖕᒍᓕᑕᖅᕙᖅ
FINAL BLOCK

ᑖᓐᓇ ᐊᑐᐃᖅ ᑭᖕᒍᓕᑕᖅᕙᖅ
ᐊᖅᑭᕐᓯᒪᕐᕙᑎᓕᖅᑐᖅ ᐃᑉᑐᐊᓕᕐᒍᑦ.
ᐊᕓᓂᑕᒻᒪ ᐊᖅᑭᑕᑎᐊᕈᐊᖅᑲᕐᖁᖅᑐᖅ
ᐃᓂᓂᐊᖅᑐᖅ ᐊᑉᑐᐊᑎᐊᑉᒐᓇᖅᑕᒍ
ᑕᒪᐃᒻᓄᑦ

The final block is set in place like a keystone. It is shaped so that it makes contact with the edges of each of the other blocks.

19

ᐅᑕᓯᒃᓴᐃᓂᖅ
FILLING GAPS

ᐃᑯᓴᓈᑯᕐᑯᑦ ᐊᐅᕕᑦ ᐊᖂᓄᖕᑎᑎᑐᒡ ᐊᖕᓗᓂᖅᐱᔪᐱᖕᐅᓖᕐᑦ. ᐅᑕᓯᒃᓴᐃᓂᐊᓪᑐᓂ ᐃᓗᖕᖄ ᐱᑐᒋᐊᑦᕐᑦ

There are likely to be some gaps between a few of your blocks. These gaps are sometimes too large. If that is the case, use the following technique to fill them.

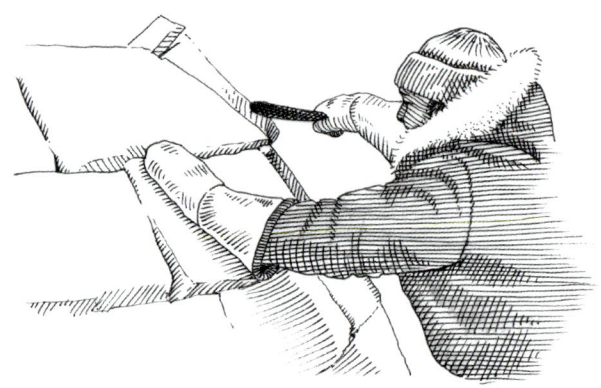

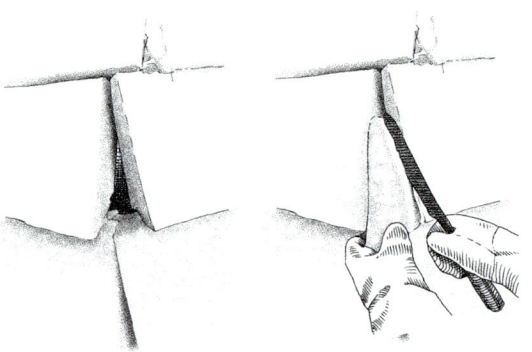

1 ᐅᑕᓯᕆᒃᑕᑎᕆᐊᖅᑕᑕᐃᑦ ᐊᖕᑎᓂᖅᖄᐅᔦᑐᓛᑐᒍ ᐊᖕᓚᕗᐊᓂᑦ. ᐸᑎᒻᒐᓗᒍ ᑭᕈᑕᐊᒍᖕᓗ ᐃᑕᖕᖂᖅᐸᖕᑐᑕᐊᓗᒍ ᐃᓄᖅᓕᑦ ᓇᖅᐸᖕᖕᑐᑕᐊᒍᓗ.

Cut a piece of snow a little larger than the gap. Hold it in place and slowly trim the edges while pushing it into the gap.

2 ᐃᓄᖅᓕᑦ ᐊᖅᑭᖅᖕᐸᖕᑐᑕᐊᖕᓂᖅᖕᓕᑦ ᐅᑕᓯᕆᕐᒃᑎᑎᒋᔭᐃᑦ.

The piece will work its way into the gap and seal it off.

ᐃᓗᐊᑕ ᓴᓂᖐ
INTERIOR WALLS

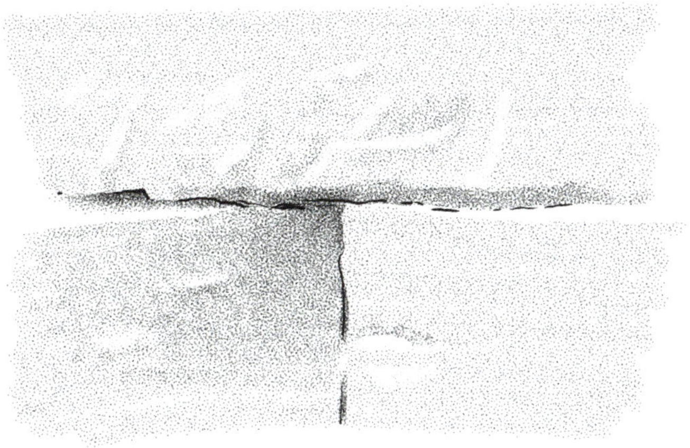

ᐊᐅᕕᖅ ᐃᓗᖕᒧᖕᒐᔩᕈᓂ ᑯᑐᒎᓂᖅᓴᐅᒐᔪᖅᑐᖅ
ᐃᓗᒻᒧᑦ ᐅᖅᑰᓯᒃᐸᑦ ᐃᒡᓗᕕᒐᖅ

A block that overlaps the row below it will produce water droplets when the iglu warms up, which will fall onto people below.

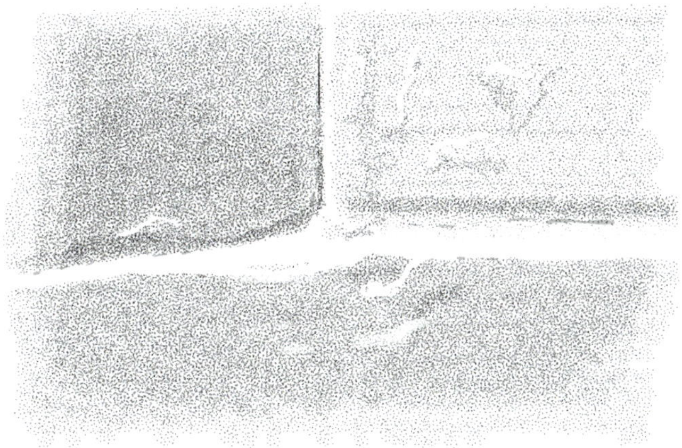

ᐃᓗᑦᑕᐅᓗᐊᖅᑕᐃᓕᒪᕆᐊᖅᑲᖅᑐᑦ ᑯᑐᒎᑯᓇᒍ
ᐃᓗᒻᒧᑦ

Ensuring the blocks are inset from the row below it will allow any water droplets to run down the walls of the iglu to the floor.

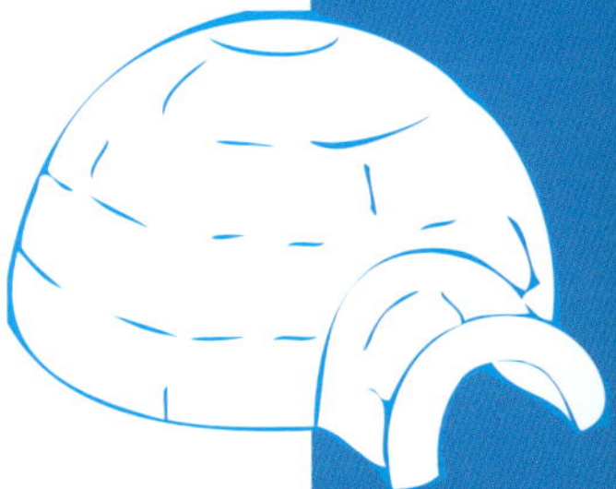

ᖅᐅᔨᒪᖕᓂᐊᑎᒡ ᐱᔪᖁᒍᐳᑕᐤᖅᖬᑐᑦᓗ
TIPS AND TRICKS

ᐊᐳᐱᖕᔨᓴᖅ:
ᐊᐳᐱᖕᔨᓚᓂ ᐃᖅᐅᒪᒉᐊᖅᖬᑐᖅ ᓗᒍᒍ
ᖅᑦᑦᐊᓂᖕᑎᓇᐊᖅᖬᑐᖅ. ᖅᑦᑦᐊᓂᖕᔨᖅᐸᖕᑲᖕᒍᐊᑉᖕᓂ ᐊᐳᐱᖅ
ᐱᖕᕆᐅᕆᑎᖕᔨᐊᕆᖅᖪᖅᑐᖅ ᐃᓂᑉᔨᖕᓗᓂᑦ.

ᑐᖕᓚᐱᐊᖕᑦᑐᑦ ᐊᐳᖅᑦ:
ᑐᖕᓚᐱᐊᖕᑦᑐᑦ ᒪᓂᖅᑯᒍ ᐊᖕᑐᐊᖕᑦ ᓗᒍᒍ
ᐅᐱᖕᓕᖕᑎᐊᖅᖬᑐᑦ. ᑕᐱᒪᐃᓂᖕᓗᖕᐸᑦ ᑭᖕᔨᓂᖕᒥᑦ ᑕᒃᑯᐊ
ᒪᑦᑦᖕᓂᓂᐅᖕᔨᐊᖕᑖᖕᓕᑕ ᐃᓯᒪᖕᓂᑦ.

ᐊᓂᖅᕼᔪᑎᖕᓂᓗ ᑲᖕᕆᐊ (ᖅᐱᖕᓗᖕ):
ᐃᑉᓗᐊᓕᖅ ᑲᖕᑎᖕᑦᖕᑎᐊᐱᐊᖅᖬᑐᖅ
(ᖅᐱᖕᓗᖕᑎᖕᐊᐱᐊᖅᖬᑐᖅ) ᐊᖕᓚᑉᐊᖕᔨᖕᓚᖕᓂ
ᐊᒉᒍᑦ ᐊᐳᓗᑦᑦᐅᑐᖅ ᑲᖕᑎᖕᖕᖭᓯᓚᖕᓂ ᖅᑯᑦᖕᖕᔨᐊᒍᑦ.
ᐱᔨᓂᐊᖅᒪᓕᖕᑭᖕᒃᑐᖅ ᐅᖅᒃᔨᐅᖕᑎᖕᖬᖕᓂᐊᑐᐊᖕᓗᓂ ᖅᑦᖕᓚᑦᖕᕈᖕ
ᔨᖕᒋᖕᓗᖕᓂᐊᖕᓂᑦ.

ᓇᖕᐅᖕᓂᑉᔨᖕᓚ ᐃᑉᓗᐊᓕᐅᖕ:
ᐅᐱᖕᓕᔨᖅᑐᖕ ᐃᑉᓗᑐᐅᖕᖕᐊᐳᑦ
ᐊᑦᖕᖕᖕᓂᖕᓗᔨᖅᑲᓂᐊᖅᖬᑐᖅ. ᐅᖕᒍᐊᓚᐅᖕᕐᓗᒍ ᐊᓚᑎᐳᖕ
ᐅᖅᑦᑯᓂᖕᓂᖕᖕᑲᖕᓂᓗᓂᑦ.

Cutting Blocks:
When cutting blocks, remember that they should be slightly wider at the top than at the bottom. If you do not angle your saw to allow for this, you will not be able to remove the block from the snow.

First Row:
When spiralling the first row of blocks from the ground slowly upward, remember to also tilt them slightly inward. Following this angle with subsequent blocks will naturally create a dome shape for the iglu.

Ventilation:
Make sure that your iglu is properly ventilated by making sure there is a vent at the bottom of your iglu and a vent near the top. This is extremely important if you plan on lighting a qulliq or a stove.

Iglu Placement:
If you are building your iglu on a slight slope, make sure that the full height of the first spiralling row is on the downward side. Place your doorway facing away from the windward side.

ᖃᒧᑏᒃ

© RON WASSINK

© RON WASSINK

ᐅᑭᐅᖅᑕᖅᑐᒥᐊᓄᑦ **ᖃᒧᑏᑦ** ᐊᑐᖅᑕᐅᔫᑎᐊᖅᒻᒪᓂᖕᔭᒃᒥᖃᒃ.
ᐊᶜᶜᶴᓇ°ᓐᖅᑐᓐᖅ, ᐊᵡᐃᐅ°ᓐᒻᓇᖅᑐᓐᖅ
ᐱᕈᓇᐅᑦᒻᓇᐃᐅᶜᑐᓐᶜᔭ ᑕᐃᒪ°°ᓕᓄᶜ.

The **qamutiik** is an essential tool in the far north. Its versatility, unique construction, and dependability have allowed it to endure over time.

ᖃᐅᔨᒪᔭᐅᓂᖓ

ᖃᒧᑎᐅᖃᑦᑕᐅᖅᓯᒪᓪᓱᑎᒃ ᓴᐅᓂᐊᓂᖅᓂᒃ,
ᑎᕆᔭᒧᖅᑯᕕᐊᓂᖅᓂᓪᓗ ᖅᐸᔪᓂᒃ, ᓇᔭᐊᓂᖅᓂᒃ, ᐊᒃᓗᖅᒥᓪᓗ
ᓇᑦᑎᕆᔭᖅᓂᒃ. ᖃᒧᑎᖅᐸᑕᐅᖅᐳᒃ ᐃᖃᓗᐊᓂᖅᓂᒃ
ᖅᑯᐊᓂᒃ ᐸᑎᓯᑎᕆᔭᐅᑐᓂᒃ ᐊᒡᒥᓄᒃ ᑲᐅᒪᓄᑕᔫᓄᒃ.
ᐱᐊᖅᓴᐅᑎᖅᖃᖅᐸᑕᐅᖅᐳᒃ ᐃᔪᖅᔭᒪᖅᓱᑐ ᓱᒻᖅᓴᔭᓂᒃᑐᓪᓗ,
ᐊᓯᐅᑦᓯᖅᓂ ᑐᓕᐊᓂᖅᓂᖅᓂᒃ ᐱᓴᖅᖅᐸᑕᐅᑎᓐᑎᑎᓐᒃ
ᐱᐊᖅᓴᖅᓯᒪᓄᒐ. ᖃᒧᑎᖅᐊᖅᔪᒃ ᐊᖅᖅᓇᐊᑎᖅᓯᒪᖃᖅᐳᒃ
ᐅᖅᐸᐊᑦᔭᖅᓄᑐ ᐅᕆᔭᐊᑦᖅᓂᓐᒃ ᐱᓴᑎᓐᑎᓕᒃᖅᓂᒃ
ᐃᓐᖅᓂᓗ ᐅᖃᕆᐅᖃᑐᒃ ᓯᑯᒃᑕᒃ ᓄᓇᒃᑕᒃ.
ᖅᑭᒧᔭᐅᑕᐅᐯᑕᐅᖅᐳᒃ ᐃᓂᐊᖅᓂ ᐃᓄᐃᔪᐊᕐᖅᓄᒃ
ᐅᓄᐊᖅᑕᐅᐯᖅᓄᒐ. ᐊᖅᖅᐳᑕᒍᑎᐊᖅᑎᑕᐅᓯᖅᑕᐅᖅᐳᒃ
ᖃᐅᑕᒫᑎᐊᖅ ᐊᑐᔪᐊᑎᐊᖅᒍᑐᒃ
ᐊᖅᑯᒃ ᔪᑕᐅᓕᔪᐊᒃᑐᒃ.

ᐅᑦᔪᒥ ᔪᑕ ᓴᒪᓂᖅᑎᐊᓐᐊᑎᐊᖅᐳᒃ
ᖃᐅᔨᒪᑎᐊᓐᐊᑎᐊᖅᓂᓪᓗ ᐊᖅᐳᖅᓯᒪᓂᖓ
ᐊᔭᔅᖅᓯᒪᓪᐊᑎᓂᓗ ᓴᓇᔅᔭᐅᖅᑐᑐᖅᒐᓐᒃ.
ᓄᓇᖅᑲᓂᒃᖅᓂᖅᑐᒃ ᐊᔭᔪᐊᖅᐊᔅᔭᐅᒃᖅᒪᒃ ᖃᒧᑎᐅᔪᔭᖅᖅᖅᐸᖅᐳᒃ
ᐊᑐᑎᓐᒃᖅᓇᒪᓄᒃᓗ ᐊᖅᑯᒃᑕᐅᔪᒐᔭᖅᑐᓂ.
ᓴᓇᔅᑎᔪᒐᔭᖅᐸᖅᐳᒃ ᖅᑭᒐᑐᐊᖅᑎᒃᑕᐃᑎᓐᒃᓱ,
ᐊᖅᖅᑭᒧᔭᐊᖅᐊᒐᔅᑐᒃᒍ ᓗᑕᒃᖅᔭᐅᑕᐅᐯᖃᖅᓂᓄ.
ᓇᐅᑕᖅᔅᑕᐅᔭᓐᔪᒃᖅ ᐊᒃᓗᒃᒐᒃᔪ ᖀᖃᒃᑐᓕᐅᐊᑎᖅ
ᖅᑭᒐᑐᐊᔅᑕᓇᒍ ᐊᖅᖅᓇᐊᔅᑕᓇᒍᒐ
ᓗᑕᒃᖅᔭᐅᑎᑕᐅᐯᖕᒪᑐ ᐅᑭᐅᖅᑕᖅᒍᒥᖅ. ᐊᑕᓇ
ᓇᐅᔭᐅᓂᖓ ᐊᑐᖅᑕᐅᔭᒪᖅᓂ ᖅᑭᑕᐃᖂᔪᐊᖅᑯ
ᐅᐊᓇᖅᒐᔭᓂᖅᒐᒐᓄᒃ.

BACKGROUND

Early qamutiik frames were made from
whalebone, driftwood, antlers, and sealskin rope.
The runners were made from frozen fish held
together with frozen caribou or walrus skin.
The running surface was prepared from either
moistened moss, covered in layers of ice, or the
rib of a bowhead whale, covered in ice. It was an
art to build a sturdy but light qamutiik in order to
haul belongings and people over huge distances
of ice and snow. These sleds were hauled by
dogs and sometimes by people. Maintenance of
these sleds was done every day to keep them
performing well in the harshest of conditions.

Today's qamutiiks still require a lot of skill to build
and are based on the same principles as earlier
sleds. There are many different variations of
qamutiiks, depending on the region of the North
in which they are being used. The principle of the
qamutiik is for it not to be rigid, but to be able to
flex and move with the surface of the ice. Tying
the qamutiik with rope rather than nails or screws
allows for this flexibility and durability, which
is essential in the harsh and rough
conditions of the Arctic. This
account describes the steps
used in the construction of
a North Baffin qamutiik.

ᐅᑕᔭᖕᖕᐱᐃᓂᖅ
SHAPE RUNNERS

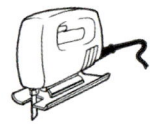

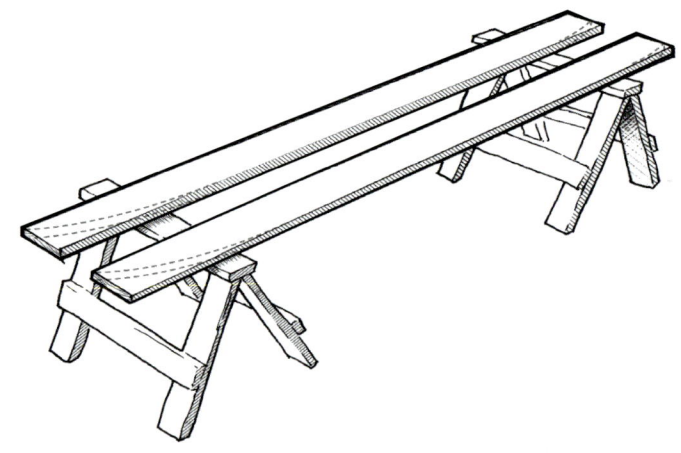

ᐊᖅᖃᖅᔭᒪᓂᓕᔭᖅᑕᖕᓛᕐᑕ ᑭᓛᒍᔾᒍᓛᑕ. ᐅᐃᓱᓂᖕᓛ ᐃᖅᖂᐊᓗ
ᐊᖅᖃᖃᑕᐅᔾᓗᔾᒥᖐᓯᑦ ᐊᑐᖅᑕᐅᖅᖃᑦᑕᑦᖐᓂᓕᔭᖅᑕᖕᓂᓄᑦ.

Rough out the shape of the runners with a skill
saw or jigsaw. The shape of the front and rear is
dependent on ice and snow conditions.

ᐸᖕᖃᖕᑕᓗᖏᖕ
JOIN RUNNERS

ᑭᑭᐊᖕᖕᐊᔾᖕᓗᑦ ᐸᖕᖃᖕᔭᒃᐱᐃᕋᑉᖐᒃᐱᕋᒃᖃᖕᓂᓗᑦ.

Temporarily join the runners together with spikes.

ᐅᕕᖕᒐᔮᓕᖅᑎᑦᑐᒋᒃ ᖃᒧᑎᒃᓵᒃ
ANGLE RUNNERS

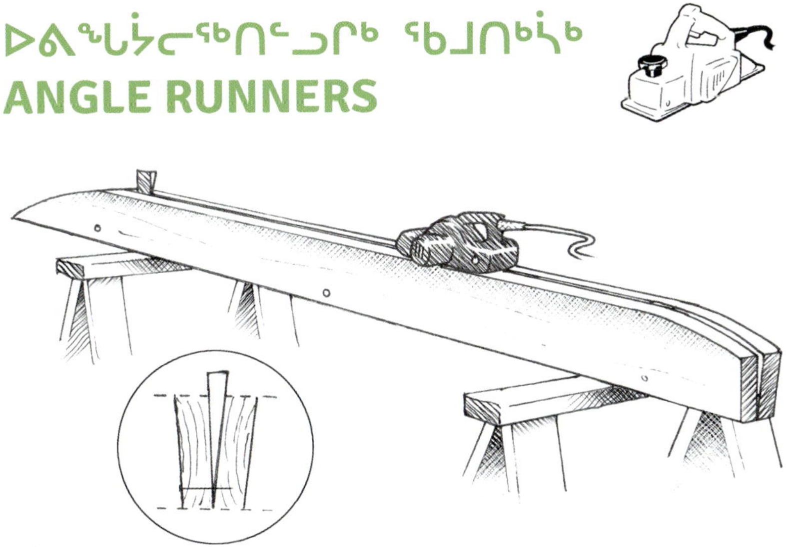

ᖁᖁᖕᒪᔪᒥᒃ ᐊᑯᓐᓂᖕᒪᓇᐊᖅᓯᓗᑎᑦ ᐊᓗᖕᒫᖕᒪᓇᑦ. ᐃᓚᐅᖅᑖᕈᑎᒧᑦ ᓇᓚᖅᑲᓈᓚᖅᑎᑦᑐᒍ ᐊᓗᐊ ᖄᖕᒪᓗ.

Insert wedges into the bottom seam of the two runners. Using a plane, flatten out the top and bottom surfaces to angle the runners.

ᐅᐃᕐᓂᐊ
SHAPE FRONT

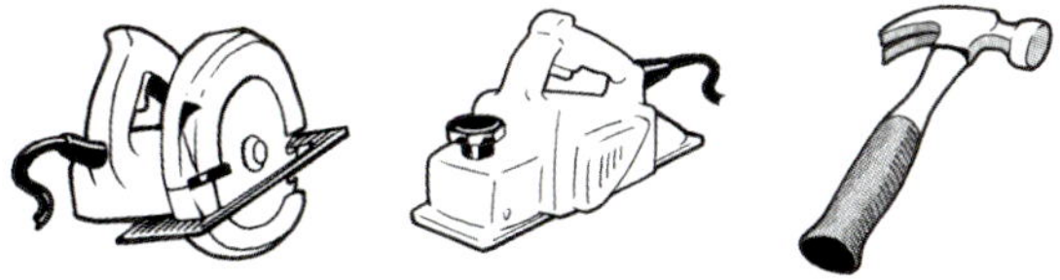

ᐅᐃᕐᓂᓚᐊᕆᔭᖅᐱᑦ ᐃᓚᕐᓂᑯᐊ ᓯᕗᓂᐊᑕ ᖄᖕᒪᓇᐊᕐᓗᒍ ᐊᑦᑐᖏᕐᓗᒍᓗ. ᖃᐃᖅᑲᒃᓴᑦᑎᐊᕐᓗᒍ ᐃᓚᐅᖅᑖᕈᑎᒧᑦ.

Separate the runners and, using the piece you cut off the bottom, fasten it to the top. Shape the front using the skill saw and plane.

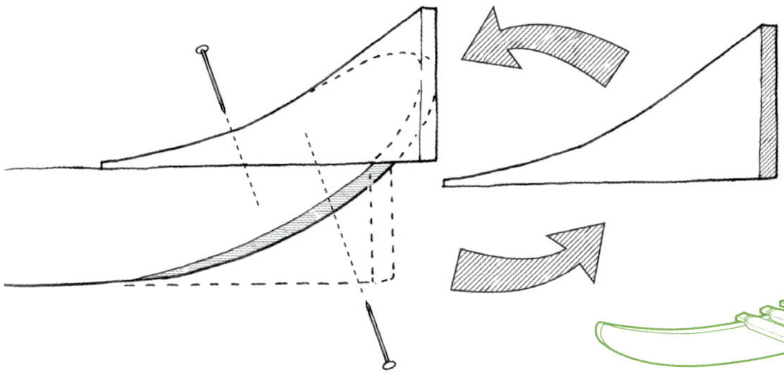

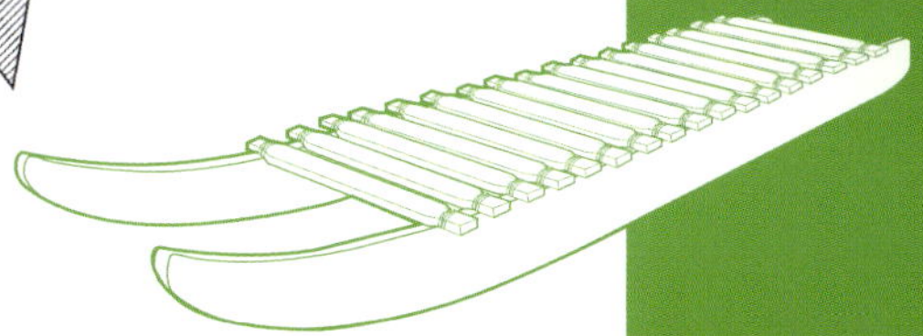

ᐅᐃᑦᓂᖕᒥᒃ ᖅᐱᖅᒋᑕᕆᐊᖅᑲᓂᖕᒥᑦ
REINFORCE FRONT

ᐊᒥᖅᑲᑕᒃ ᖅᑕᖃᔪᐊᖕᕐᑐᒃ ᖅᐱᖅᒋᑦᓗ ᑭᐱᐊᒃᑐᐳᑭᐅᔓᓗ ᑭᐱᐊᑐᐃᐊᖅᐅᔓᑦ ᖅᐱᖑᑕᖁᐃᔓᑦ ᐊᑐᖕᑰᐅᔓᑐ.

Use light- or medium-gauge sheet metal to reinforce the front section of the runners. Attach with screws or ribbed nails.

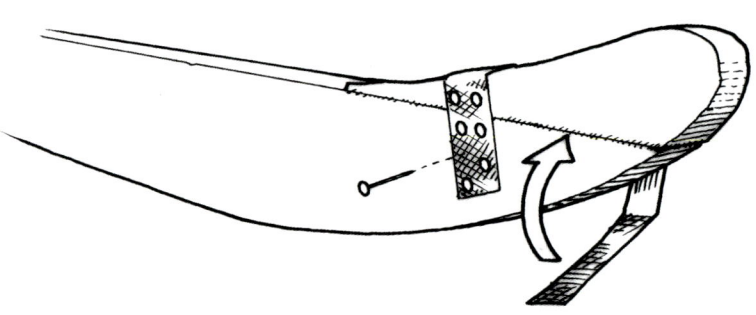

ᓇᐳᑕᐅᕆᖅᐱᖅᓱᖕᒥᑦ
DRILL HOLES

ᓇᐳᑕᐅᕆᖅᐱᑕᐅᑐᐊᖅᑐᖅ ᐊᕿᖑᔾᐊᖅ ᒪᓕᒃᑐᒍ. ᓇᓪᒎᑎᖑᐊᖃᖕᑐᒃ ᖅᑐᐱᖢᓴᐃᖁᑕᒍ. ᐊᕿᑎᖅᒃᒨᒋᑐ ᓇᐳᑕᐅᑎᖕᖔᓂᒃ ᓄᖒᓴᐃᖁᑕᒍ.

Drill holes in the runners as pictured above. Make sure the holes are offset to reduce the possibility of cracking. Round off the holes to minimize rope fraying.

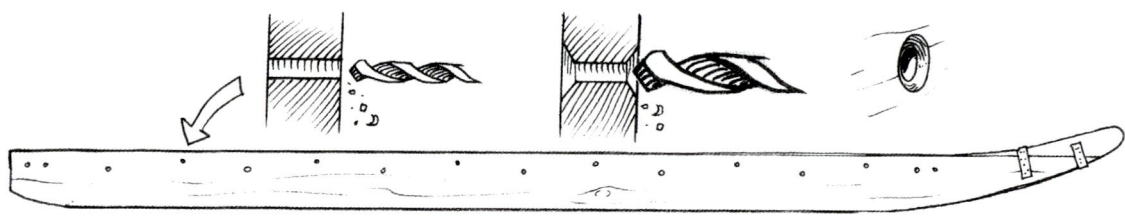

ᓇᐳᓚᐅᕐᓂᖅ
CUT NAPOOKS

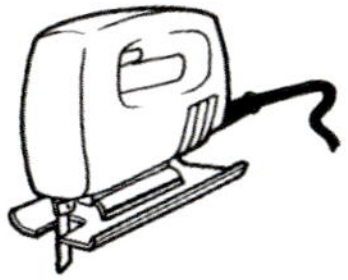

ᓇᐳᓚᐅᓯᕐᕕᒃᓴᓚᐅᕐᓗᒋᑦ. ᐊᔾᔨᒌᙱᑦᑐᓂᒃ ᓇᐳᓚᐅᕈᓯᕐᑲᐅᕈᓐᓇᖅᑐᑦ. ᑎᓴᒃᑕᐃᑦ ᐊᑦᑕᕐᓇᙱᓐᓂᖅᓴᐅᔪᓐᓇᖅᐳᑦ ᐊᑐᑐᕐᑲᐅᔭᕈᓐᓇᕐᓂᖅᓴᐅᓪᓗᑎᒡᓗ.

Cut crossmembers (napooks). There is wide variation in the shape and style of napooks. Generally hardwoods will last longer.

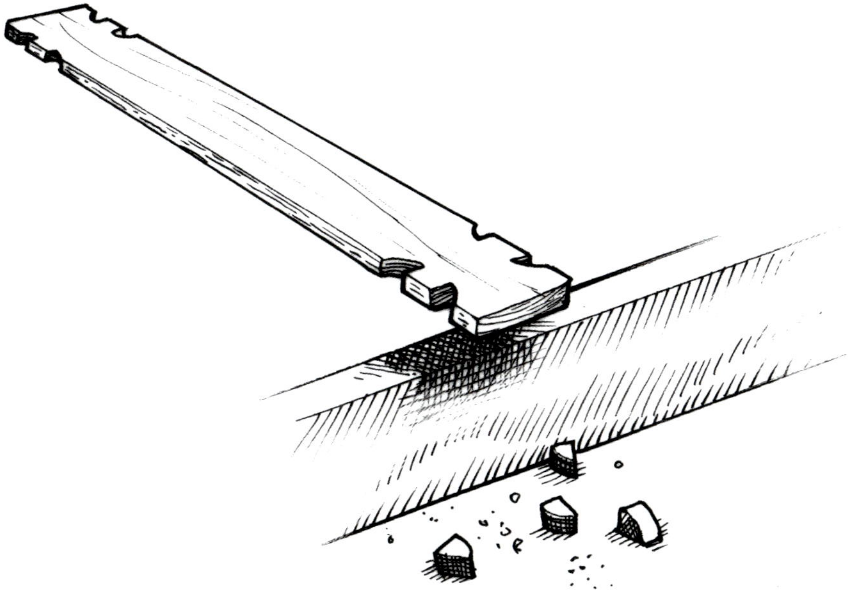

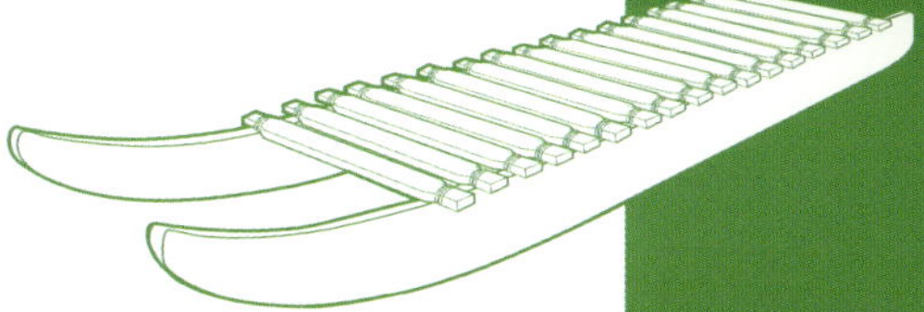

ᑫ>ᵘᒉᑕ ᠵᑫᑦᒉ─ᖅᐸᠸᖅ ᕐᖮᒍᑉ─ᖅᐸᐸᠸᠥ
FIRST/LAST NAPOOK
(ᠵᑫᠥᐊᠥ ᐃᖅᑯᐊᠥᠴ/FRONT TO BACK)

1 ᑫ>ᒉᐅᐢᑕᑦ >ᑐᵘᒋᑎᑐᑕᑦ ᒍᓌᐅᖅᠴᠴᑐ
ᑫᠥᑫᐃᖅᠵᐸᑫᑦ ᒪᒉᑦᠥᑐ.

Feed the rope through the holes
in the runners as indicated.

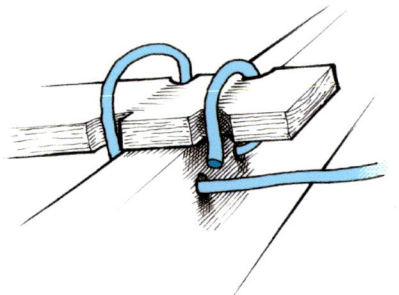

2 ᒪᠵᐳᐃᖅᠵᑳᠥᠥᠴᠴᑐ ᠵᑫᑦᑕᐅᖅᑳᐅᐸᑐᑕᑦ.
ᠵᑲᑕᕐᐃᓚᑐᑲᐅᐅᖅᠴᠴᑐ. ᐃᠵᐸᑐᑦ >ᑐᒉᐅᐅᖅᠴᑐ.

Feed the rope twice more, as in step one. Do not
tighten. Create a loop at the end of the rope.

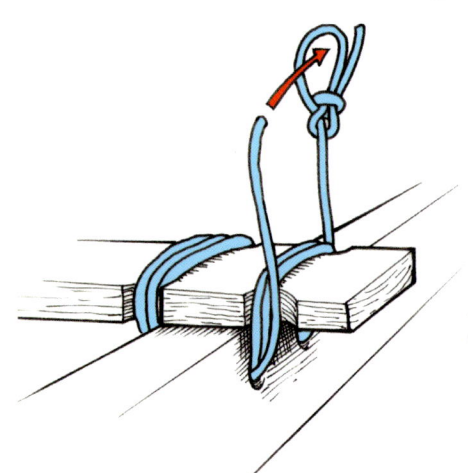

3 ᒍᓌᠴᑐ >ᑐᒉᐊᓂᠴᐨᖅᑳᐅᑕᑦ.

Feed the loose end of the rope
through the loop you created.

4 ᓯᑲᑎᖅᐸᑦᑕᐊᒍ ᖅᑲᔪᑎᖅᑦᓂᖕᖐᓂᑦ ᐱᓯᐊᔾᒍ.

Tighten the rope so that the loop is just protruding from the hole in the runner.

5 ᒪᑎᖅᐸᑦᑕᔪᒐᑦ ᖅᕐᐧᖕᓂᓂᖕᒐᑦ. ᐊᓛᓂ ᓯᑲᑎᖅᐸᑦᑕᐊᕐᓂᐊᖅᖅᑐᑦ.

Tighten the free end of the rope. You may have to tighten each round of rope separately.

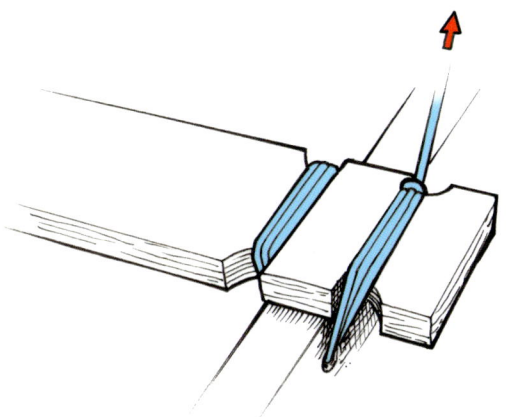

6 ᖅᐸᕐᖕᖅᔭᒃᑐᒐᑦᐧ ᐊᔪᐃᓗᒍ. ᐃᕐᐊ ᓄᐊᐅᖅᖅᓗᒍ ᐊᑐᖕᑕᐅᑎᓗᒍ ᖅᑲᓐᑐᒍᓪ

Lift the outside round of rope slightly with a screwdriver. Feed the loose end of the rope under and repeat many times. Tie off with a half-hitch knot.

ᓇᑐᑕᖅᓯᐱᐅᓂᖅ
TYING NAPOOK
(ᓯᐳᓂᐊᓂ ᐃᖅᑯᐊᓂᒍ/FRONT TO BACK)

1 ᐃᑐᖅᓱᖁᑕᐅᑦ ᓄᕕᑐᒍ.

Insert a loop into a hole from the inside of the runner.

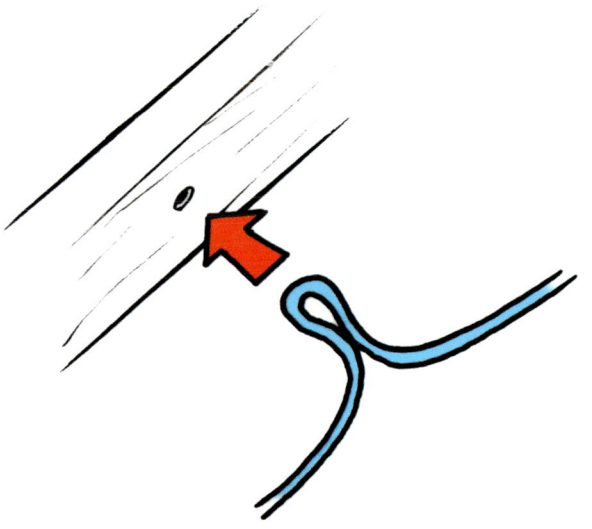

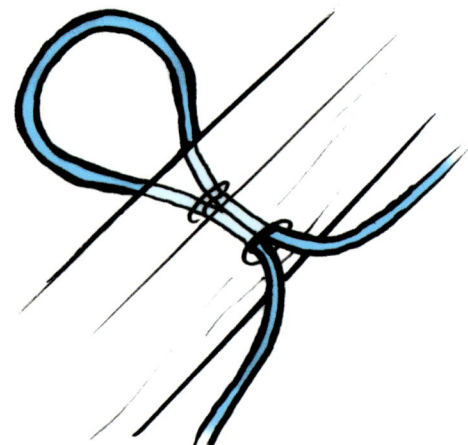

2 ᓯᓚᑖᓂᓂᖅᕿᖅ ᓂᑎᑐᑎᐊᕐᑐᒍ.

Enlarge the loop on the outside of the runner.

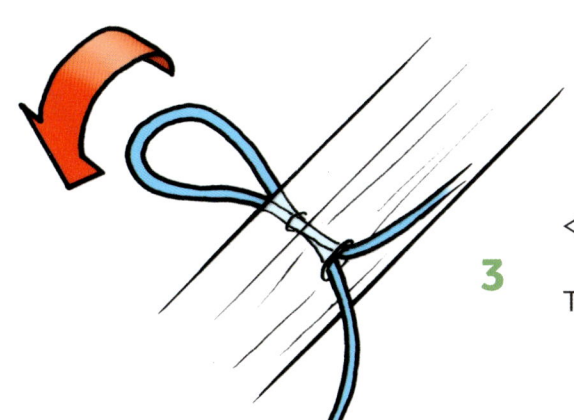

3 ⊲ᑕᐅ<ᐅᐊᖅᒍ ᑭᕐᖃᑥᒍᖅᑎᒃᒍ.

Twist the loop once.

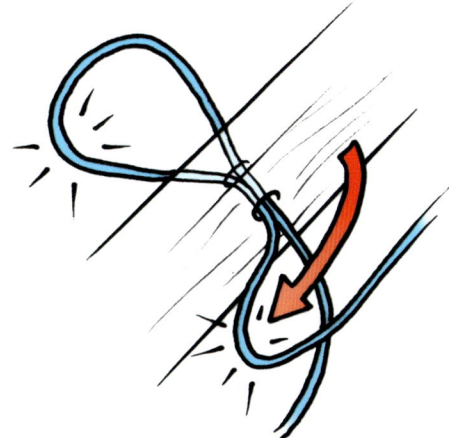

4 ᐳᑦᖃᑕᖅᑎᒃᒍ ᐃᑐᖂᖕ ᓇᑐᐊᐃᖅᕕᒪᓂᖕ
ᒪᒡᒍ. ᑎᒍᒍ ᐳᑐᑕᐅᖅᕕᒪᐊᖅ

Create a loop on the inside of the runner
as indicated. Grab the loops as indicated.

5 ᖅᑭᕐᖃᑐᖅᒍ ⊲ᑕᐅ<ᐊᖅᒍ.

Twist once, as indicated.

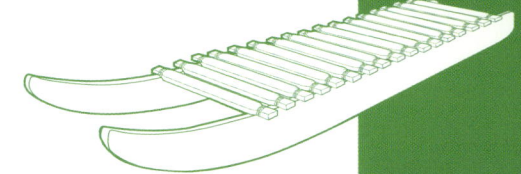

ᖃᒧᑏᒃ QAMUTIIK

6

ᕐᑯᒻᒧᒃᑎᑦᑐᒍ ᓇᐳᐊ ᐃᓗᖅᑯᖅᑐᓈᕐᑯᑦᑐᒍ.

Lift the loops in preparation for the napook.

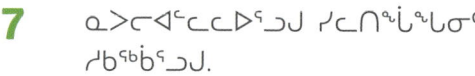

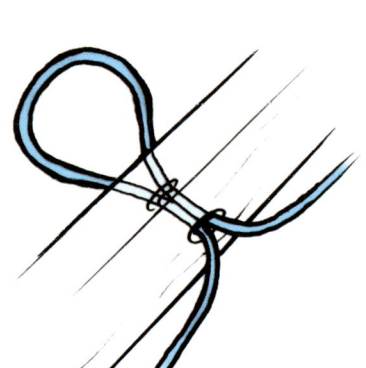

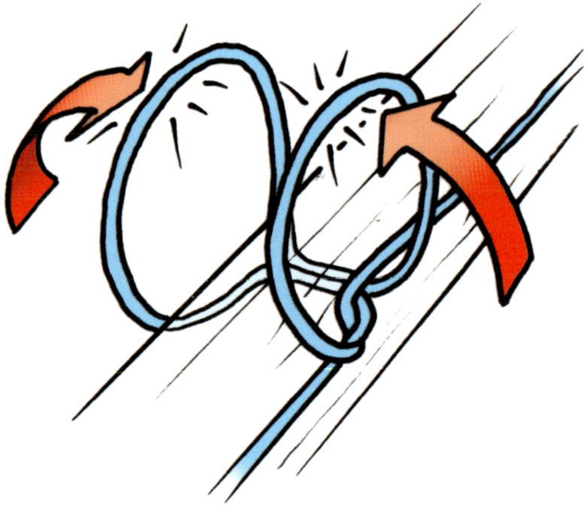

7

ᓇᐳᓕᐊᑦᓚᓚᐅᕐᑐᒍ ᓯᓚᑎᖕᒑᖕᒐᓂᑦ ᓱᑲᖅᑳᕐᑐᒍ.

Insert the napook. Tighten the outside loop first.

8

ᐃᓚᖕᒐ ᓱᑲᓕᕐᒥᑐᒍ ᓇᐳᐊ ᐊᐅᓚᑎᑦᑐᒍ ᓱᑲᑦᑎᐊᕈᓐᓇᕐᑯᑦᑐᒍ. ᓇᐳᓕᐊᑖ ᓱᑲᑦᑎᐊᕈᓂ ᐃᒻᒥᓂᒃ ᐊᑦᑐᖕᒋᐅᑎᒋᕗᖅ

Tighten remaining rope and move the napook back and forth while pulling the rope, so the napook seats itself tightly. Once tight, this knot is self-locking.

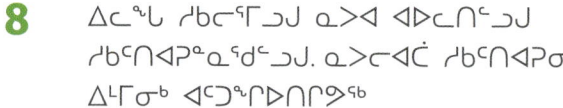

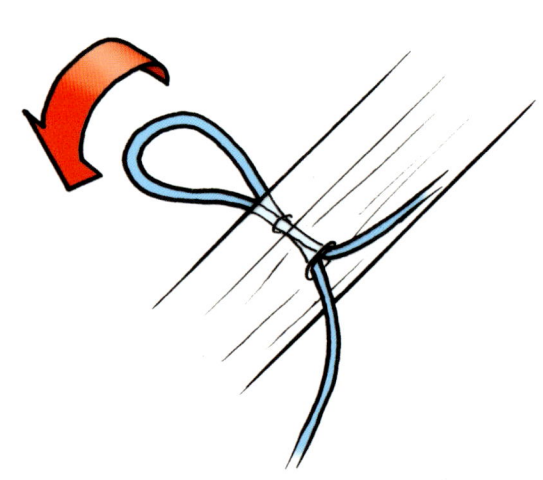

ᐱᕐᒐᖕᒥᑦ
SLIDERS

1 ᐱᕐᒐᖕᒃᖕᒥᑦ ᖃᖏᕐᓚᖕᒐᖕᒍᒃ ᑭᑭᐊᑐᖕᒐ̄ᓚᕐᑦ.
ᐃᓚᕗᓯᒥᐊᖕᖃᕐᑐᖕᒐᒃ ᐱᕐᒐᔮᖕᔪᕐᓚᓂᕐᒃᓂᑦ.

Screw nylon "sliders" to the bottom
of the runners as indicated. Make
sure that the screws are countersunk.

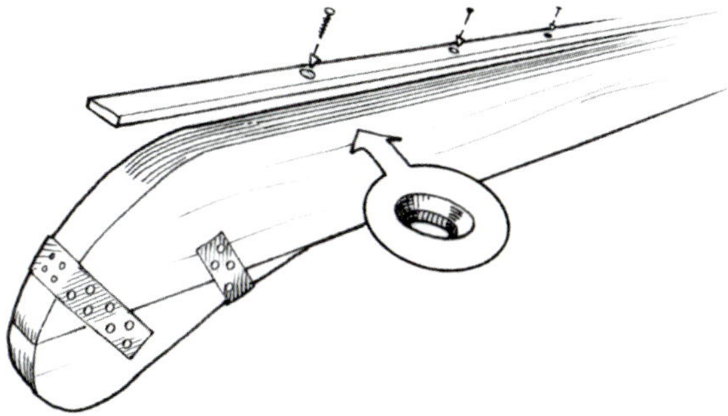

2 ᐊᒐᖕᑕᒐᔭᒃ ᐃᔭᓚᐊᖕᕐᑐ̄ᒐᒃ ᓯᖅᓇᐊ
ᖃᑕᐊᐲᕐᓚᒍ. ᐊᖕᒐᓂᖕᒃᓚᐅᓯᕯᕐᔪᖕᑫᖕᑐᖕᒃ
ᖃᑕᐊᐲᕐᐅᑎᕐᑲᐃᑦ.

Use medium-gauge sheet metal to
reinforce the "noses" of the runners.
Leave at least a three-quarter-inch
overhang on the sides.

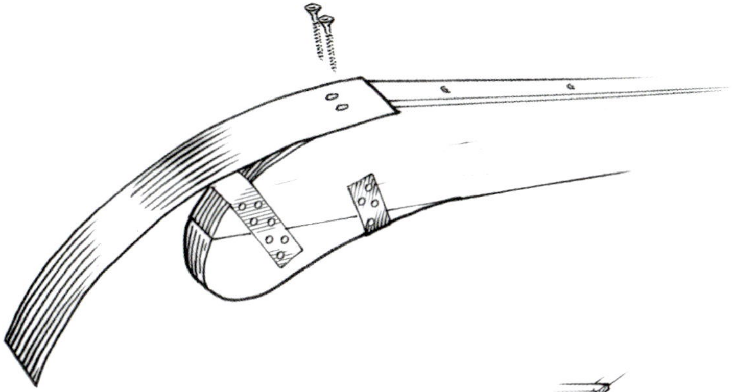

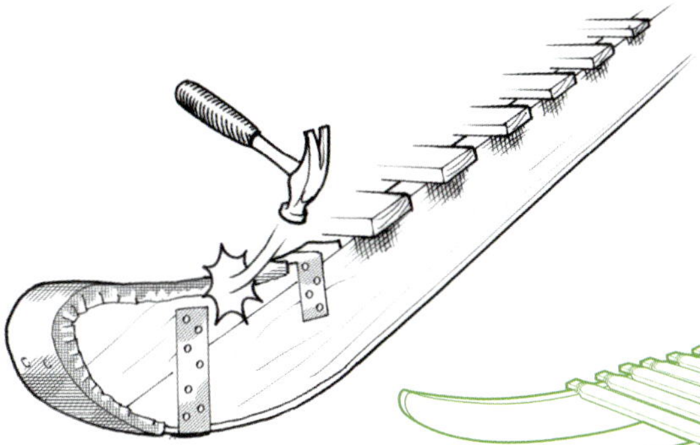

3 ᒪᖕᒃᑎᐅᖕᒃᓚᒍ ᑕᐃᒪᖃ ᑭᕐᓚᕐᓂ.

Hammer down the overhanging sheet metal
to protect the edges of the wood.

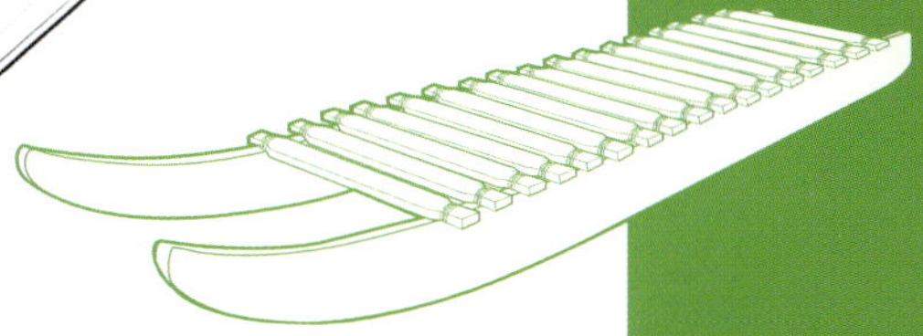

ᖃᐅᔨᒪᔭᕆᐊᓖᑦ ᐱᖕᒪᕆᐅᑦᑕᐅᖃᑦᑐᓛᑦ
TIPS AND TRICKS

ᐅᐃᓯᓂᖅ:

ᐅᐃᓯᓂᖅᒪᑕ ᖃᐅᔨᒪ ᐊᔾᐱᖕᒍᓈᖃᑦᑕᖅᑎᒐᔪᓕᑎᓪᕙᓗᖕᑐᖅᖅᐅᓈᐊ ᓗᑦᖅᑦᖃᐅᔭ-ᒪᓂᑦᖃᕐᑦᐅᑐᐸᖃᖅᐅᕝᓗᑦᖃ ᐅᐃᓯᓂᖅᐊᖅᖅᑐᓂᖅᑦᑦᕙᐅᕝᖃᖃ ᒪᓂᕋᐊᖂᓂᒐᕝᒍᕝᐅᑐᐅᕝᖃᓂᑦ ᐅᐃᓯᓄᑦᖅᐊᖃᖅᖅᖅᓂᖃᑦᑦᕙᐅᕝᔪᓂᑦ.

ᐊᑐᖅᕝᖅᑐᑦ ᖃᒍᑎᖃᕝᐅᓄᖕ:

ᖃᒍᑎᖅᕝᓂᓪᒐᕝᖃᖅᓂᑦᖃᕐᕝᓂ ᐅᕐᓄᐊᓯᓂᖃᖅᖅᑐᑦ ᖅᑦᕙᕝᖅᑦᐅᑦᓂᑦᖃᕝᑐᓂ ᐊᑐᕝᕝᖃᓂᑦᒐᕝᖃᖅᑦᕝᐅᑐᖃᕝᑐᓂᓗ

ᓇᐳᑕᐅᑎᖅᐢᕝ ᐊᖃᖂᐢᖅ:

ᓇᐳᑕᐅᑎᓂᖃᕝᖅᑕᐅᐃᑦ ᐢᓂᑦᓕᐊᐅᓕᖃᖅᖅᑎᖃᒪᖀᒐᕝ ᐃᕝᖕᕝ ᐃᕝᖃᖅᖅᖂᓂᑦ ᑐᒐᕝᓂᖅᖅᐅᑦᖃᖅᖕᖂᐅᑐ ᖃᖅᖅᑐᑐᐊᓕᐊᖃᖅᖅᐃᓂᖕ. ᖃᑐᕝᖃᐃᑦ ᓂᖅᖅᑐᑦ ᓂᑦᖅᖃᑎᐅᑎᖃᕝᖅᖅᑐᖅ ᑕᐳᖃᓂᑦᒐᕝᕝᑐᓂᓗ ᖃᒍᑎᖕᓂᑦ ᑕᐳᓂᖅᖅᐃᑕᖃᖃᒪᐅᑐ.

ᐱᓲᖁᑎᑦ:

ᓂᖃᓄᐊᑐᑦ ᐃᓚᖃᖕᖃᓂᐊᖅᖅᑐᖅ ᐊᑦᑕᖃᓄᖕᕝᓂᖃᑦᑕᐅᒐᓄᐊᖅᑐᓂᖃᖂᒍ ᐅᕝᓵᐊᖃᖅᑐᑎᖃᓂᐊᖕᓂ ᐅᖅᑯᒪᐃᓕᑐᓄᖕ. ᐱᓲᖃᒪ ᖃᒍᑎᖃᒐᕝᑦ ᓂᑦᐃᖕᖅᑐᑦᕝᐅᑐᖃᕝᑐᖃᕝᒐᕝᒐᕝ ᓄᖕᕝᒐᐃᐅᐃᕝᖂᖅᐊᓂᒍ ᖃᒍᑎᑕᖕᓕᓂᖕ.

Nose:
The curvature of the nose of the qamutiik depends on the terrain it will be used in—rough, jumbled ice requires a more curved nose, while smooth, flat ice requires a more gently sloping nose.

Wood Material:
If choosing solid wood for the runners, make sure there are no cracks or serious knots. Plywood can be used to face the runners for added strength. Hardwoods such as walnut or oak are ideal for napooks.

Rope:
For tying the napooks, use rope no thicker than a quarter of an inch, which doesn't slip on itself when tied in a knot. For a pulling rope, choose a material that doesn't stretch too much, and is at least half an inch and at least one-and-a-half times as long as the qamutiik.

Runners:
Plane the runners to about an eight-degree slope—this provides stability and strength when carrying a load. Nylon sliders should be slightly wider than the runners to prevent damage to the wood.

© RON WASSINK

ᑎᑎᕋᖅᑐᑉ ᒥᒃᓵᓄᑦ

ᓱᓗᒧᓂ ᐊᐃ ᐱᐅᕐᒪᑕᖅ ᖅᖐᒥᒋ, ᐃᒡᓗᓕᐅᑉ ᖃᓂᒋᔭᖓᓂ ᑐᖅᖅᖐᑦ/ᖄᐅᐋᖁ 2, 1959ᒥ. ᒥᑭᔪᓂᒋᒥᒃ ᐲᓯᓕᒥᒃ ᐊᐊᑎᒥᒃ ᑐᑭᓱᒍᒪᖃᑦᑕᐅᖅᑕᖅ. ᒥᖅᓱᑎᐅᑕᐅᖅᑐᖅ ᖅᒉᓂᒃ ᐊᑰᒥᒃ ᐃᓕᓐᕿᓂ, ᐊᑉᐊ ᐊᖁᒥᒃ. ᐊᑖᑕᓯᑎᐅᖅᑕᖓ ᒪᑕᐃᐊᕝ ᐊᐃ, ᓴᓇᙳᐊᖅᕆᑕᐅᑕᐅᖅᑐᖅ, ᐱᔪᐊᖅᖐᒡ ᑑᒥᖅᓂᐅ- ᐃᓕᖕᓚᓂ ᐅᐊᑎᐅᖅᑐᒥᖅ ᑐᒃᑐᑉ ᓇᒃᖓᕐᐊᓂᒃ ᐅᑰᐃᖁᐊᖅ--ᓱᓗᒋᓂᐅᑦ ᐃᓕᖓᐱᕆᓕᒃᖓᕆ ᓇᓇᙳᐊᖓᕐᒃ.

ᓱᓗᒧᓂ ᐃᖕᑎᐅᑕᐅᖅᑐᖅ ᒥᒃᔭᓕᓂ ᐃᓕᕆᔭᐅᕆᓂ ᐅᒡᓕᒥᖅᕆᑦ ᓂᕐᖓᐅᕆᖅᑎᒋᑦ. ᐊᖑᐵᖕᖅᕆᑎᒋᒃ ᓂᖅᐅᕆᕐᖔᑎᓂᒃ ᐱᖕᒍᐊᕙᖓᖅᑐᖅ, ᓱᓗᓪ ᐱᐊᒥᒃ. ᑎᑎᕋᖁᖓᖅᕆᑎᓂ ᐃᖕᑎᓕᖓᒃ ᐃᓄᒃᑎᑐᖅ. ᓇᓇᖅᑕᑦᑎᕆᕕ ᖅᑕᐅᑎᓂᒃ ᐸᐃᑎᐊᖁᓂᑦ, ᐃᓇᙰᐊᖁᓂᑦ ᐲᒃᑐᐃᖁᓇᕆᓂᖅᑐ ᐱᐺᐱᕐᑕᓂᑦ.

ᖅᑯᐃᐊᕐᕕᖅᒋᕆᕝ ᐅᓂᒃᑲᑎᐊᖅ ᐃᓕᑐᐅᖅᑎᒋᒃ ᐊᑖᑕᒥᒃ. ᐅᓂᒃᖃᖅᑕᐅᖅᑐᖅ ᐃᓂᙳᐊᖁᓂᒥ, ᓄᖀᖅᑭᐅᑕᐃᐊᓪ ᓄᓇᙵᓚᖁᖃᖁᓇᐅᑎᒋᕝᕆᖅ ᐅᓂᒃᖃᑎᐊᖅᑐᖅᑳᕆ ᑕᓗᒃᑐᙵᒃ. ᐃᓇᙳᐊᑎᑎᖅᖃᒃᑕᖅᑐᖅ ᐃᓄᐃᑦ ᐃᓕᖅᑯᓯᕐᙰᓂᒃ ᓄᐊᐕᒥ ᓯᕐᑐᑦᖐᖁᐊᖐᒥ. ᐃᖅᖃᓇᐃᖅᑐᖅ ᖅᐱᖅᑕᓂ ᐃᓄᐃᑦ ᑲᑐᔾᖄᖅᑎᑦᙰᕆᓂ.

ABOUT THE AUTHOR

Solomon Awa was born in a sod house near Iglulik on November 2, 1959. From a young age, he was curious about everything around him. He learned to sew traditional items such as seal skins from his late mother, Appia Awa. His late father, Mathias Awa, was an excellent carver, especially with ivory—one time he made a harpoon from caribou antlers in one night—and Solomon learned to carve from him.

Solomon started singing at a young age in a contemporary band. He plays many instruments, including organ, and writes songs in Inuktitut. He also handcrafts drums for daycares, local schools, and various other places.

He loves to tell the stories that he learned from his father. He does this at schools, and also had the opportunity to go to Kaotokeno, Norway to tell some of these stories. He teaches traditional knowledge at Nunavut Arctic College and works for the Qikiqtani Inuit Association.

© RON WASSINK